The

and prayers.
May God continue
to bless you.

Eph 3:19

Deep Spiritual Thoughts

Trevor Feltham

WESTBOW·
PRESS
A DIVISION OF THOMAS NELSON
& ZONDERVAN

Holy Bible, New International Version. Grand Rapids, Michigan: Zondervan, 1985, 1995, 2002. Hereafter referred to as NIV.

Holy Bible, New Living Translation. Carol Stream, Illinois: Tyndale House Publishers Inc., 1996, 2004, 2007. Hereafter referred to as NLT.

The Voice Bible. Nashville, Tennessee: Thomas Nelson Inc., 2012. Hereafter referred to as The Voice.

Laubach, Frank, and Brother Lawrence. *Practicing His Presence*. Jacksonville, Florida: The Seed Sowers, 1973.

Peterson, Eugene H. *The Message: The Bible in Contemporary Language*. Colorado Springs: Nav Press, 2002. Hereafter referred to as MSG.

WestBow Press books may be ordered through booksellers or by contacting:

WestBow Press
A Division of Thomas Nelson & Zondervan
1663 Liberty Drive
Bloomington, IN 47403
www.westbowpress.com
1 (866) 928-1240

ISBN: 978-1-4908-6609-3 (sc)
ISBN: 978-1-4908-6611-6 (hc)
ISBN: 978-1-4908-6610-9 (e)

Library of Congress Control Number: 2015900455

Printed in the United States of America.

WestBow Press rev. date: 01/14/2015

This book is dedicated to friends and family who have encouraged me on this journey. Specifically I would like to thank my wife, Trilbi, and our three kids, Coulson, Julia, and Jordan (listed from oldest to youngest). Trilbi has taught me more and more about what it means to love. The way she loves and cares for me and our family is inspiring. I am learning how to love from her example. Our three kids also inspire me in many ways. Our conversations and the way we hang out and learn from each other are motivational. Doing life with them has taught me much about many areas. I love them all.

Introduction

Deep Spiritual Thoughts is the name I have chosen for this book. I might have called it *A Relentless Pursuit of God* or *Practicing the Presence of God*, but I decided on this title as each numbered entry represents much deep thought pertaining to spiritual matters. I know this is not earthshaking, but that is what happened. I could have said I received insights from God while I was alone with Him in the wilderness for 365 days, but that would not be true. This book got started one day as I was seeking God in my prayer time. I had an idea that started out with a general statement. *You know*, Trevor, I told myself, *a year is not a very long time.* I looked back over the last year and previous years and agreed that indeed a year is a short time. I then examined how I had spent my time over that last year and realized I had wasted a lot of it. I realized that if I took that wasted time and spent it seeking God and practicing being in His presence, I might be a much different person in one year. I was right, and the insights that resulted form the contents of this book.

Growing up in a pastor's home, I came to know Christ at an early age. I then spent the bulk of my teenage years running from Him and getting into everything that I should have avoided, from drugs and alcohol, to promiscuous relationships, to theft. I thank God for saving me from where I was heading. I was saved, or resaved, and returned to the fold. I then felt a strong call to pursue youth ministry, so I entered Bible college. While there, I learned a lot about God, theology, and relationships. This small college strongly encouraged matrimony. The norm was to find your spouse and head into ministry. I bought into this hook, line, and sinker. I got married while in college and started working in youth ministry upon graduation. I was involved in this field for a while, but things went south at the church where I worked, and there were few options for youth pastors in my denomination since most churches were small. I did the next best thing: I went into sales.

I worked for a resort company and quickly moved into management. I started making lots of money and thought I was all that and a bag of chips (sea salt and malt vinegar, of course). However, deep down in my soul I felt a tug from God to become a senior pastor. I took all the necessary steps and started the process with ministry boards and district superintendents. I was then appointed to my first church. The church was between pastors, and this was supposed to be a six-month interim appointment. It turned into three years.

I learned a lot about ministry in those three years. Unfortunately, my approach in those early days was to kick down the doors for Christ. I was a mover and a shaker, and I was going to make stuff happen in ministry. "This is what I plan to do for You in ministry," I told God. "Would You please bless it?" I have learned that this approach was all backward and that God has to lead the ministry. Jesus has to walk before me, beside me, and behind me. It has to be His cause, not a cause that I pick and ask Him to bless. I learned this the hard way. I went to a second church to attempt what is called a "turnaround." That was a district superintendent's way of saying, "Let's go to this old church and revive it. Let's get young people involved and create a vibrant church for Christ." That sounded good to me. Unfortunately, I found a group of older people who didn't have the energy to reach out to new families and didn't want to change the way things were always done. This was a futile effort since once again I was trying to do things my own way and not waiting on God to see what He wanted. I remained at this church for a couple of years. I was then called to a young, happening church with a full worship band and thought this was going to be awesome. Unfortunately, family stresses made a productive ministry impossible. One thing led to another, and I ended up having to leave the ministry sooner rather than later.

What now? I had little choice. I received no help from the church or from the district, so I packed up my family (I had two young sons by this time) and moved across the country. I returned to the resort industry, started over again in sales, and was promoted to manager in a short time. If I couldn't be in full-time ministry, then I was going to make lots of money. That is what I did, among other things. I woke up one day and found myself divorced and back into drinking and drugs. I guess old habits really do die hard and tend to resurface during our weakest moments. I was living day to day, numbing my pain with alcohol and drugs. *How did I get to this point?* I wondered. I am not proud of this seven-year period but felt justified as I was going through it. I thought the church offered no help whatsoever, so I turned my back on the church for a few years. I needed something to shake me out of this. That something came late in 2011.

I was managing a team of salespeople at a high-end resort, and one day the president walked into my office and sat down. He told me that the company was in trouble and was shutting down sales that day. The workday was coming to a close, so we were finishing up with our last clients. He had me call a team meeting at which he broke the news to the staff. I was shocked, and so was my team. We had families to support. What would we do? Apparently the ownership was broke and couldn't pay us any severance. The company was involved in litigation, and we got no money. This was the eye opener that I needed to start my painful journey back to God. I had two boys to support, so

I decided to take a job at a resort all the way across the country. This would be a fresh start.

We got rid of all our furniture and most of our possessions. We moved with two suitcases and shipped one box each. The boxes contained keepsakes, and the suitcases held our clothes. That was it. I started seeking God and never stopped. I thank God every day that He is a God of restoration. He not only restored my faith in the next couple of years, but He restored the faith of my boys and arranged the perfect partner for me, whom I later married. God did a lot of work in my heart, and now I do things His way. All my decisions include a consultation with Him. If I am not sure of something, I wait on God, and He guides me. This book is about the thoughts that God has given me throughout this process. When I started seeking Him, I wanted to do an experiment that lasted 365 days. I decided to take the time to be in God's presence, to listen to what He had to say to me, and to write it down. The deep spiritual thoughts in this book are a result of my intense year with God as recorded in my daily journal. This story is not over.

The latest chapter was a health scare. While I was on a holiday on the East Coast, I learned from my family doctor that I had a form of cancer. He told me that when I got back I should see a hematologist, who could better diagnose me. For a month I thought I had cancer, and that was scary. When I returned I saw the specialist and he informed me that I chronic lymphocytic leukemia. At least it was in an early stage. I faced yet another challenge: how would I get healthy again? I learned a great deal about diet and changed all my eating habits. I learned that an alkaline body is much healthier than an acidic body and that my body was highly acidic. Slowly but surely I am changing that with God's help. In all my struggles, I am now sure that God will support me. I feel peace, knowing that everything will be all right. After my intense year in God's presence, I now understand that nothing is impossible for Him and that He is at work in my life, causing great things to happen. I am seeing Scripture come alive in front of me and the greatness of God everywhere.

I hope that these writings will cause many to seek God intensely and that they will create their own disciplines as they practice His presence. I pray this will happen, all for the glory of God. To Him be the glory forever and ever. Amen.

The Prejourney

I am preparing my mind to be in God's presence for the next 365 days. The first lesson I have to learn is to stop trying and to allow God. As silly as this sounds, I am trying to stop trying. I am learning to focus on God and to let Him guide me. For twenty-five years I have been trying to do God's will my way, but I might as well have been banging my head against a cement wall. It doesn't work.

I am having a hard time with the flesh. I am contemplating the things I will have to give up if I am to succeed in concentrating on God's presence for the next 365 days. Alas, I am still missing the point. This process isn't about giving up stuff out of duty. It is about having an ongoing connection with God so He can reorient my flesh. I cannot do this on my own. I will always struggle with the flesh, but I have a feeling that as I draw closer to God, I will want the things of the flesh less and want Him more. The ideal is a moment-by-moment connection with God through which all my ideas are actually His.

I am learning that I have made the gospel much more difficult than it is. In fact, the gospel is all about God. As I approach the challenge of being in God's presence for the next 365 days, I feel fear. I am filled with doubt, asking myself if I can pull this off and do my part. I know God will do His part if I will only stay the course and do mine.

Several questions come to mind.

Does God really want a moment-by-moment relationship with me?

Is He really here with me all the time?

How is that possible?

I know deep down that He indeed wants such a relationship and is always with me. I believe, but going forward, God, would you help me in my unbelief?

These are normal fears that I want God to help me overcome. These 365 days of practicing His presence will be quite a ride. As you read these passages, I hope they encourage you to strive for a deeper relationship with God. May you find Him in these thoughts. Whether you read and meditate on one thought per day or more than one at a time, may you have a blessed time with God.

Press on...

Life in the Mundane

This was the first day of my spiritual deepening as I sought God's presence. I had been a Christian for quite some time, but I had been running from God for seven years. I would go to church on occasion, say a few prayers when I was in trouble, and pretend I was a Christian. I was good at pretending, but I was only fooling myself.

I had been a pastor for ten years, five as a youth pastor and five as lead pastor. I thought I had all the answers to the problems of the church and of the world. Boy, was I arrogant—and wrong. God had to take me through the refining fires and many painful years of wandering in the wilderness to get me to where I am now.

And where is that? Simply a place where I now experience God's presence more than I ever have. God is showing me things about myself that are painful but true. My attitudes, my thoughts, and my lifestyle choices are all put up for scrutiny. I repeated King David's prayer to God, asking Him to search me and to know my heart. If you read Psalm 139, you will begin to see just how much God knows you, especially if you reflect upon the psalm verse by verse, thanking Him as you do.

From there, I started my journal with the intent of writing something every day for the next year, even if it was that I had learned nothing that day. Ah, life in the spiritually mundane! That is often the result, but looking back, I can see that in those dry days, in those days of silence, there was growth. I believe God teaches us truths and then allows time for these truths to sink in. He knows we forget easily and need reminding often. That said, here are my thoughts from my first day of journaling.

For many years I have been searching for a deeper relationship with God. I have searched in the wrong areas and with flawed methods. This was my fault, not God's. I blamed Him for the circumstances leading to my leaving the pastoral ministry. How could God let those things happen? I pulled away from Him and from the church. Looking back, this was ironic. I was doing this when I most needed God and the church. I should have been listening to James, who said that if we draw near to God, He will draw near to us. I was doing the opposite.

The first day was an interesting one, mainly orienting me in my connection with God. I set up hourly reminders on my cell phone to pray, to read Scripture, or to place my mind on God or the things of God. Nothing mind-blowing took place. I simply got used to doing things a different way in the mundane.

Life is lived in the mundane. In fact, we spend much more time in life's routines than on spiritual peaks or in valleys. If we could see the mundane as an opportunity, we would be ahead of the game. In the mundane we can reflect on how great God is and recount the many victories He has won on our behalf. Let's be thankful for the mundane. Every time I think of the mundane, I am reminded of a passage in Romans. I believe *The Message* translates it best. Here is what it says.

"So here's what I want you to do, God helping you: take your everyday, ordinary life—your sleeping, eating, going to work, and walking around life—and place it before God as an offering. Embracing what God does for you is the best thing you can do for Him. Don't become so well-adjusted to your culture that you fit into it without even thinking. Instead, fix your attention on God. You'll be changed from the inside out. Readily recognize what

He wants from you, and quickly respond to it. Unlike the culture around you, always dragging you down to its level of immaturity, God brings the best out of you, develops well-formed maturity in you" (Romans 12:1–2 MSG).

Embrace the mundane.

Press on...

DEEP SPIRITUAL THOUGHT #212

That Bloody Love

I started day two by writing that it was a new dawn and that I wanted the second half of my life to have more meaning than the first and to make a significant contribution to the kingdom. I was already into big-picture thinking, which usually gets me into trouble. Having been on this journaling adventure for two whole days, it was time for me to go out and change the world or at least to allow God to change the world through me. The pattern for me is to get a neat thought from God about a spiritual truth and then to feel an immediate and insatiable desire to connect that to the larger picture.

In my early ministry days I was a little zealous. My mentality was, let's storm the hill for Jesus. My approach this time is still a little zealous, but I have been given wisdom enough to ask, Does Jesus want to take that hill by storm? Good question. After twenty-five years of trying to kick down doors, I have finally realized that Christ will walk before me and unlock, open, and even hold the door for me to walk through. Interesting! My thinking has changed since I have been on this journaling adventure.

I went from shouting, "Let's take the hill," to saying, "I want nothing to do with the church," to asking, "God, what role do You want me to play in Your kingdom work? Where are You leading me? Where are you beating a path for me and lighting it with Your Word?" These are the questions that will make a difference in my spiritual walk and in my service to Jesus. I had great intentions when I was storming the hill, but I was always motivated by my interpretation of what God wanted. Now it is God's interpretation of what He wants. If something isn't clear, I wait on God and trust in His Word. Before I was quite sure God would be okay if I did this or that for His kingdom; after all, I was doing it in His name.

The biggest lesson I have learned is to get ego out of the way, to understand that everything is about God, not me, and to act accordingly. At this point in my life, when I am asked if I would ever go back into full-time ministry, I can confidently say, "If that is where God is leading me, that is what I will do." I now know that He will be leading me. A year ago I was still saying I would never return to any form of ministry. I am not sure what the future holds, but a year of getting to know God makes a huge difference. My life is not about me in the least. I still struggle with that, and suppose I always will, this side of heaven. In any case, I want to live the second half of my life to the fullest.

One of my prayers throughout the year has been from Ephesians 3:14–21, Paul's prayer for spiritual growth for everyone who is a believer and who will be a believer. My focus has been on living life to the full and on understanding what it means to have this fullness of life and where that comes from. Verse 19 is a favorite that I cling to: "May you experience the love of Christ, though it is too great to fully understand. Then you will be made complete with all the fullness of life and power that comes from God" (Ephesians 3:19 NLT).

Experiencing God's love leads to fullness of life, and it comes with the resurrection. This is the finished power that raised Jesus from death. That is what I want in my life, but not so I can do great things and people will say, "Wow! Look at what Trevor did." I want people to say, "How did God restore Trevor to a point where He is using him in this way? Wow! God is great. Without God, Trevor is nothing."

All you need is love. It covers a multitude of sins. Since I started quoting this verse to myself, I have been asking God to allow me to experience this love so I can be more effective at showing love. One of the most important things Christians can do is simply show more love. They will know we are Christians by our love—not by how impressive we are but by how impressively we love. Love is the answer for the world. This is not misguided love or love that comes from the flesh but agape, God's love. His love brought Jesus into a crazy world so that He could take our place on a criminal's cross and die for us. That is ultimate love. That is blood love. That is the type of love that will change the world. That is the type of love that lets us experience the fullness of life and the power that comes from God. We can experience and share this love only because He loved us first. This is the love I want to experience. Then all the other types of love—with a partner, family, friends, and other Christians—become not only possible but probable.

That is how I want to live my life. That is why I am seeking God's presence. That is why I choose to offer my body as a living sacrifice. The second half of my life will have a greater impact than the first because that love was made available to me. It is written, and it is finished. That blood love is available to me today and every day. When we experience that type of love, our behavior starts to change. When this love fills our hearts, much love will flow out. Now when facing a dilemma, instead of asking, *What would Jesus do?*, I ask, *How would Jesus love?* The answer I receive is much more profound and usually catches me off guard. However, the more I practice this love in complete openness and honesty, the more God takes care of the results.

I am no relationship expert, but I now understand that the key is not understanding with your mind. That is only the first part.

You have to ask the right questions. God does the work through you when you allow His love to overflow.

> When I think of all this, I fall to my knees and pray to the Father, the Creator of everything in heaven and on earth. I pray that from his glorious, unlimited resources he will empower you with inner strength through his Spirit. Then Christ will make his home in your hearts as you trust in him. Your roots will grow down into God's love and keep you strong. And may you have the power to understand, as all God's people should, how wide, how long, how high, and how deep his love is. May you experience the love of Christ, though it is too great to understand fully. Then you will be made complete with all the fullness of life and power that comes from God. Now all glory to God, who is able, through his mighty power at work within us, to accomplish infinitely more than we might ask or think. Glory to him in the church and in Christ Jesus through all generations forever and ever! Amen. (Ephesians 3:14–21 NLT)

Press on...

What Me Worry?

Did you ever read *Mad* magazine as a kid? If so, then you will remember Alfred E. Neuman, the magazine's mascot, who appeared on the cover. His mantra was, "What, me worry?" I can still see his red hair, chubby cheeks, and freckles. He seemed to imply that there was no need to worry, that he could relax, knowing everything would be all right. At least that was the case for Alfred E. Neuman. Can the rest of us believe this nonsense? No need to worry? That is silly. If you are even a little bit human, you have probably come up with a different answer. You may say, "That's definitely not me. I worry about everything." Or perhaps you may say, "I sometimes worry about things. I know I shouldn't, but I am only human." You may think that this human quality justifies worry. Does it? Let's look at the question from a different angle and from a more authoritative source than *Mad* magazine.

"Don't worry about anything: Instead pray about everything. Tell God what you need, and thank Him for all He has done. Then you will experience God's peace, which exceeds anything we can understand. His peace will guard your hearts and minds as you live in Christ Jesus" (Philippians 4:6–7 NLT).

What, me worry?

Three words stand out right away for me in this passage from Scripture. The first is *anything*. Don't worry about anything.

These are Paul's instructions to us. Yep, that definitely takes in a whole lot of territory. The next word is *everything*, as in "pray about everything." Everything covers all subjects. Paul is saying that no matter how big or how small the issue or the concern, you must pray about it.

The next word, *then*, ties the first two together. If we do the first part, then we will experience the peace that passes all understanding in our hearts. The first two words involve things of the mind—worry and prayer. When an anything enters our minds, we pray about it, and it becomes a part of the everything. These things also involve the heart, but the mind is where anythings, including worries, usually start. We gain God's peace when we get this one right, and who wouldn't want a big old slice of that peace? After all, it does pass all understanding.

As I looked more closely at this Scripture passage, a fourth word jumped out at me. This word sums up how we find that peace. The word is *thank*. Thank God for all He has done, and then you will find His peace. Anything, everything, thank, peace—awesome!

This peace serves another function. Verse 7 says His peace will guard our hearts and our minds as we live in Christ Jesus. That is the goal: to be living in Christ Jesus, to be so close to Him that He will guard our hearts and our minds from anything and everything. That is the formula for peace that passes all of our human understanding. Think about the most peaceful thing you can. Perhaps you are lying in a meadow with beautiful flowers all around you, the aroma tantalizing your nose, the sun beaming on your face, the clouds floating by in neat pictures that seem to tell a story. You think to yourself, *Now that would be peaceful.* The peace that Paul talks about goes way beyond that. No matter how far we stretch our imaginations, we still won't get there. The peace that is available when we live in Christ Jesus exceeds anything that we can understand. That is the kind of peace that I want.

Don't worry about anything.

Pray about everything. Tell God what you need.

Thank Him for all He has done.

Then He will allow you to experience the peace that passes all understanding.

Your heart and your mind will be guarded when you live in Christ Jesus.

Who wants a piece of that peace? I do.

What, me worry?

Press on...

The Real Four-Letter F-Word

Cast all your anxiety on him because he cares for you.
—1 Peter 5:7 NIV

The four-letter F-word keeps me out of God's will. It throws me off of my path. It has the potential to freeze me in my tracks, to make me second-guess my decisions, and to cause me to miss a journey that may be God-led. That F-word is *fear*. You have probably heard the acronym FEAR many times. It stands for False Evidence Appearing Real. That is fear. It rarely involves anything that has yet happened. So why does it have such a grip over us? Why is it easy to understand intellectually but hard to overcome spiritually? Why is it difficult to cast all of our anxieties on the God who cares for us and leave them with Him?

The formula is simple, but the practice is oh so difficult. The formula is to stay connected to God's Spirit moment by moment and He will take care of the rest. It is extremely difficult to be connected to God and anxious and full of fear at the same time. This causes a cognitive dissonance in your brain, which cannot hold two conflicting ideas at the same time, and you will go crazy. If you remain connected to God day by day, hour by hour, moment by moment, then you will bear fruit.

We face many fears. I feared my experiment would not bring me closer to God. At times I feel my soul is cold. I have been a Christian for more than twenty-five years and have spent ten years in pastoral ministry, but I always misread God's will. I was doing my will, thinking it was from Him, and as a result one of my fears for the second half of my life is that it will be filled with disappointments and messes similar to the first half. I prayed, "God help me do Your will Your way. Help me to experience the greatest adventure of my life by living out of a moment-by-moment connection with You. God, I know that I cannot control the future and for sure cannot change my past, but help me to live faithfully with You right now. Help me to follow up this moment with another moment and another and another until I have one full day of living in Your presence. Help me to follow up that day with another day, then another until eventually it becomes a week. Help me to stretch that week into a month and then into a lifestyle that becomes the formula for the second half of my life."

Frank Laubach's story seems all too familiar to me. In his first forty-five years, he lived a pretty average life. He was an American-born Christian living in a remote part of the Philippines. On his forty-sixth birthday, he wrote in his journal, "I no longer have the sense that life is before me, as I had a few years ago. Some of it is behind—and a miserable poor part it is … This present moment, if it is full of God, is the only refuge I have from poisonous disappointment and even almost rebellion against God." But that was not the end of Laubach's story. In fact, it was only the beginning.

He wrote this in 1930, the year he started his deepened journey and his journaling. His transformation gives me hope that the second half of my life will be much more meaningful than the first. That has been my prayer for the past year and continues to be. God is working to bring meaning to my life, even using my past to produce good. God has an amazing ability to yield good from brokenness.

Many who have written about Laubach have said little about his spiritual life because they did not understand it. The journal entries appearing in *Practicing His Presence* were taken from letters written by Laubach to his father from 1930 to 1932, titled *Letters by a Modern Mystic*. In January 1930, he wrote, "Two years ago a profound dissatisfaction led me to begin trying to line up my actions with the will of God about every fifteen minutes or every half hour ... It is clear that this is exactly what Jesus was doing all day every day ... It is exactly that moment by moment surrender, responsiveness, obedience, sensitiveness, pliability, lost in his love, that I desire to explore with all my might" (Laubach 1973, 2–3).

Excerpt from January 29, 1930:

"I feel simply carried along each hour, doing my part in a plan which is far beyond myself. My part is to live this hour in continuous inner conversation with God and in perfect responsiveness to his will" (5).

Excerpts from April 19, 1930; May 14 and 19, 1930:

"The experiment is interesting, although I'm not very successful thus far. The thought of God slips out of my sight for I suppose two-thirds of every day, thus far ... yet this thing of keeping in constant touch with God ... is the most amazing thing I ever ran across. It is working ... this concentration upon God is strenuous, but everything else has ceased to be so ... I worry about nothing, and lose no sleep" (14–16).

Excerpt from September 21, 1930:

"It is difficult to convey to another the joy of having broken into the new sea of realizing God's hereness ... When He gives Himself He is giving more than anything else in the universe" (22).

Excerpt from October 12, 1930:

"How I wish, wish, wish that a dozen or more persons who are trying to hold God endlessly in mind would all write their experiences so that each would know what the other was finding as a result. The results, I think, would astound the world" (22–23).

Laubach was an interesting man. He was a missionary and an educator and was most famous for his "each one teach one" literacy program, which has been used to teach approximately sixty million people to read in their own language. Laubach was responsible for much more concerning education and is the only American missionary to be honored on a postage stamp. Laubach knew the presence of God and seemed to understand the concept of living life to the full.

This is the eternal quality of living that flows from a life lived in a moment-by-moment connection with the living God. This is life to the full. That is what the Bible means by abundant life, living above what we see in this world, living above the fears and concerns of the day, living above financial and health worries. Living abundantly contradicts what society teaches.

Laubach's challenge started me on my own experiment. I would seek God for 365 days and would journal about my results. These writings represent some of them. Seeking God moment by moment has changed my thinking on many levels, and the results have amazed me. The formula for abundant living is to seek God, to form a moment-by-moment relationship with Him, and to trust Him in obedient living. I felt the challenge after reading what Laubach wrote about spending a year in God's presence. Two things stood out for me in his account.

"I want to understand the joy of having broken into the new sea of realizing God's hereness." Throughout my Christian journey I have desired that deep sense of God's presence. I heard other people, mostly church leaders and authors, talk about this and thought they were fakes because they lived differently from what they said. I had tried repeatedly to enter God's presence in that intense manner but never got there. I think my motivations were wrong. As a result of my experiences, I concluded that church leaders were simply saying what they were supposed to say to encourage their followers to have a close relationship with God. I certainly didn't see the abundant life lived out often. I am sure that some of these people are fakes, but not all of them. Some have experienced God's presence in that abundant living way. Some are swimming in the "new sea of God's hereness." That's where I want to be. Jump in with me. The water's fine!

The second part of the challenge is a corporate call to this experience. What would happen if a dozen or so people did this and shared their experiences? The results, as Laubach said, "would astound the world." So again, jump in with me. The water's fine!

What is stopping us from living our lives out of this moment-by-moment experience of God's presence? My challenge was to practice God's presence for 365 days and to journal about it, and during this process God has taught me a great deal about who He is. I continue to learn each day, and my prayer is to grow even closer, to continue to learn who God is, and to live daily in His presence. When fear comes knocking, I need to let it know that love reigns here and that perfect love casts out all fear.

> God is love. When we take up permanent residence in a life of love, we live in God and God lives in us. This way, love has the run of the house, becomes at home and mature in us, so that we're free of worry on Judgment Day—our standing in the world is identical with Christ's. There is no room in love for fear. Well-formed love banishes fear. Since fear is crippling, a fearful life—fear of death, fear of judgment—is one not yet fully formed in love. We, though, are going to love—love and be loved. First we were loved, now we love. He loved us first. (1 John 4:17–19 MSG)

Press on...

Prayer: What Is It Good for? (Absolutely Everything)

Prayer is probably one of the most misused tools in our spiritual arsenal, but it has the potential to change the world. What is it good for? Absolutely everything. My problem with prayer is that I am always looking for shortcuts, and I tend to do silly things like fall asleep when I am praying. I often get involved in grocery-list prayers when what I really want is a deeper connection with God. Prayer is how that happens. Prayer should not be one-sided but should be conversational. I do a lot of listening in prayer. That is what I hope to get across in this note.

This is not meant to bash or put down anyone. Rather my advice comes as a result of my own lack of success in prayer.

E. M. Bounds was a great American preacher and a writer whose works were widely sought after. He lived from 1835 to 1913. Bounds once wrote, "Man is looking for better methods. God is looking for better men." Like many people of faith, he knew that unless you have God's ear through prayer and faith, you have nothing that can change the world. These people knew that prayer changes stuff. We think we know that today, but do we experience it? If we do, why don't we share more of our prayer stories with each other? We would grow together in faith if we shared more about how God rescued us, healed us, or gave us a neat insight through prayer. Is there power in our prayers today? Do we know what the term "fire from heaven" means in relation to prayer? Is the Holy Spirit's presence so intense when we pray that we sense things are going to change? Are we changed as a result of prayer or of being in God's presence? Why do we believe mightily in prayer but spend little time doing it? Are we too busy? These are all questions that I have asked myself over and over.

Many people have probably asked the next question. Does prayer feel like doing nothing, making it appear to be an insignificant ministry? I have been caught up in that lie. After all, there are so many more important ministries, right? Because of their seeming unimportance, do we hurry through our prayers, making sure we get everything in? Or do we wait on God and practice His presence, no matter how long that may take?

These are all great questions that I find myself asking.

Bounds said that man is looking for better methods. That seems to be a pattern in society. Technology helps us to move forward with better methods all the time. This is a part of our culture. If we aren't moving forward, we are falling behind. We need faster and better, at least in the technological world. We seem to treat prayer the same as we do technology, whereas we should be praying slowly and deliberately with a focus on knowing God more and being known more by God.

Bound also said that God is looking for better men. He is looking for people who want to know what it means to be in His presence, no matter how long that takes. When we are in His presence, we have better methods. We become God's methods.

Do we rest too much in our own strength? Do we feel a false sense of security as if we don't need God? Do we believe that God can still perform miraculous signs as He did in the past? Or do we not care about the supernatural as much today as long as our fridge is full, we have gas in the car, a good job, and a nice place to live? Do we say that it would be neat to see God do miracles, but if we don't, we don't, and who has time for that?

Why aren't many people desperate for God? Or do we fail to recognize their desperation because it appears different today?

We need to revisit this thing called prayer. We must realize as Christians and as the church that the world is a much better place when God's people are crying out to Him in prayer. The more forces fighting evil in the spiritual realm the better. Do we believe in a spiritual realm with evil forces and demons, or has all that ugly stuff been too watered down by Hollywood and society to be believable anymore? I don't know. Just asking.

We need to relearn that prayer is multifaceted. Prayer can act as a purifier, keeping evil at bay and defeated. It can and does act as a healer—physically, mentally, emotionally, and spiritually. Prayer can prevent what could happen if evil were left alone. Prayer is a daily conversation with God. It is also an urgent plea for God to change our destiny from hell to heaven. Prayer can produce peace in war, order in chaos, love in the midst of evil.

Prayer is a panacea for what is wrong with the world today. We need to get down on our knees and experience the power of renewed prayer for the sake of the kingdom, so help us God!

Remember, "Come near to God, and He will come near to you" (James 4:8 NIV).

"The Lord looks down from heaven on all mankind to see if there are any who understand, any who seek God" (Psalm 14:2 NIV).

Prayer is practicing God's presence.

Press and pray on.

Was It a Dream or a Reality?

Disclaimer: This is not meant to put down social media. Social media outlets are not bad in themselves, only when they are abused, much like anything else. The point is that we need more human touch and interaction.

I have been having weird dreams lately—dreams that are philosophical in nature, dreams that speak to life as it is lived today. I am not sure if this relates just to me or if it also pertains to the general populace. As I was waking from a dream this morning, I felt myself heading for a Rick Mercer–style rant. My dream involved several people who were going through the day having one empty conversation after another. I started thinking about this and the why behind it. I made a shocking discovery that won't surprise most people. We are in danger of losing our ability to have deep, meaningful conversations.

This was a scary and sobering thought. So I reflected on this to see where I was concerning the problem. I get up, go to work, and involve myself in a discussion about TV shows people may or may not have seen. Around the water cooler, that progresses to weather and to sports talk—depending on what playoffs are happening and who is left in the running. (For me, no Maple Leafs, little talk.) We seem to have lists of topics that we will discuss throughout the day. They may also involve music or fashion and will veer off course depending on lifestyle, whether you have kids, and other interests.

We spend a lot of time at work. Do we need to have similar conversations every day, or can we break through the shallowness of small talk?

We also have conversations on Facebook. We will ask other people to check out a recipe, a picture, or a point of interest that few care about. "Come and play the latest game with me," we will say, and if others don't, we will still keep inviting them.

Then we may jump on Twitter to see what's going on only to learn a long-lost buddy whom we hadn't heard from in years had bacon and eggs for breakfast this morning. Checking our business connections, we go to LinkedIn and find we have ten pending recommendations from people we don't know. "Look how good I am," we are telling others. "I bet I can build a better profile than you so good companies will read it and desperately want to hire me." If you look at other social media sites, you will get similar results.

The reality is that most people visit these sites precisely for such shallowness. To empty their minds from a stressful day at work, they go on to play a game or two. That is okay until it becomes all they do and all their interaction is wrapped up in social media.

After doing this for a while, people say, "I need to take a break from social media." Their souls cry out to be fed.

Social media sites have lessened our ability to have the meaningful conversations that everyone needs from time to time, conversations that are just plain good for the soul. So the challenge today is to have a deep, meaningful conversation with someone. (Or if that fails, at least a semi-deep and meaningful conversation. Remember that Rome wasn't built in a day.) Share with someone a concern, open up, or be a shoulder to cry on for another person. That is what makes us real people. That is what people are missing in their lives, and that is what people are crying out for in this shallow society. Make the most of all your conversation opportunities. You will be glad you did, and someone else will be glad you did.

Be someone's inspiration today! Do it!

Press on...

DEEP SPIRITUAL THOUGHT #314

The Intimacy Is in the Whisper

"Go out and stand before me on the mountain," the Lord told Elijah. And as he stood there, the Lord passed by, and a mighty windstorm hit the mountain. This terrible blast tore the rocks loose, but the Lord was not in the wind. After the wind there was an earthquake, but the Lord was not in the earthquake.

"And after the earthquake there was a fire, but the Lord was not in the fire. And after the fire there was the sound of a gentle whisper" (1 Kings 19:11–12 NLT).

Today I am learning about listening to God. We have many distractions in our world, and since God speaks to us mostly in a whisper, it is hard to hear unless we are tuned in (connected moment by moment). Why does God mostly whisper?

I have come up with a possible reason. First, the most important thing is that we listen. Are we listening actively or passively. Are we intent on hearing the voice of God, or do we have the TV going and the music blaring when we are trying to listen to God? So the first point concerns our listening skills and our willingness to quiet our hearts, to be still, and to know.

The second observation I have made has to do with being engaged in an intimate relationship. When two people are angry at each other, they usually show it and perhaps yell and scream a little. You yell and scream just a little bit, don't you? I know I do. This is about distance, not in space and time but in intimacy. People involved in an argument aren't seeing eye to eye or soul to soul. When you are in a disagreement with someone, you feel far apart from this person and you tend to care more about being right or getting your point of view across, things pertaining to the ego. With a parent and a child this is a little different. Sometimes we yell and scream because our kids can't hear us or choose not to hear us. What happens when you disagree with someone close to you in matters of the soul? The volume seems to come down because the disagreement is not about the ego but about genuine concern.

The more intimate we are with someone, the less volume we seem to need in our discussions. The more intimate we are, the gentler and quieter we are. Since God loves us so much and longs to have an intimate relationship with us, He tends to speak softly to us so we will be drawn more into His presence. Our part is to draw near to Him, and He will draw near to us. The closer we are drawn into His presence, the more we enjoy the quiet intimacy of His beauty. We will hear the whisper and be thankful that He isn't yelling at us. If God does raise His voice to us, it is usually because we are in deep trouble, are not hearing Him, or have done something terribly wrong and have ticked Him off. God help us if that is the case.

I am more and more thankful that God chooses to speak softly and tenderly. He calls us in an intimate way. This is a great example of how we should treat the ones we love—gently and lovingly, not angrily and with yelling. We tend to resort to shouting and anger when we are out of sync with God or when our defenses are down, for instance when we are tired. We tend at those times to revert to our natural mode. What a great thing it would be if we didn't have to respond in this mode. The only way of avoiding this is by becoming more intimate with God, by drawing nearer to Him so He will draw nearer to us. Then our natural responses will be overtaken by the supernatural, and we will start to change our default mode. The more intimate we are with God, the more we can become intimate with each other. That is a great message for the world. Jesus is still the answer. To take that a step further, intimacy with Jesus is the answer for Christians today so they can in turn share that intimacy with their world.

We must return to that moment-by-moment connection in God's presence. The more we connect with God on that basis, the more clearly we hear His voice. The more we hear His voice, the more we do His will. The more we do His will, the more we hear His whispers. That is the cycle of life to the full. When we are in that intimate state with God, we finally come alive in terms of our purpose. When we hear God's whispers and respond in obedience to His will, we start to live the abundant life. Like anything, this takes discipline and practice. I wish I could hear God's voice more. I wish it were audible. But how intimate would that be? The intimacy is in the whisper!

The next time I wonder why I can't hear God, I need to remember it's because He isn't yelling at me, which is a good thing. He is simply inviting me to enjoy an intimate, moment-by-moment relationship in His presence. The next step for me after understanding that the intimacy is in the whisper is living in this intimacy. I am not naturally good at intimacy, so I need to listen intently to what God is telling me and to act on it right away. I find that when I get these quiet thoughts from God and act in obedience, I grow spiritually and want to continue and deepen that intimacy.

God, teach me how to be intimate to the point of hearing Your quiet whispers in my ears. Help me to understand it is You and to act on the whispers. Take away all the fears associated with acting out of obedience. Help me to love intimately the way You love intimately. My eyes are open, my heart is open, and my soul is open. Come, Lord Jesus. Let's be intimate.

Remember: the intimacy is in the whisper!

Press on...

Back to the Future, God Style

I was awakened this morning by a song on "The Gospel Greats" program. I have my alarm set to a Christian radio station, which is a great way to wake up. The first thing to enter my subconscious mind in the morning when I am not quite awake is Christian music or a Scripture verse. The song was about God being in control of our future. I thought, *Wait a minute. God is already in my future.*

Whenever I feel fear for the future, I need to remind myself that God is already there waiting for me. He is in a situation before I arrive. That truth resonated deep within my spirit. A sense of peace washed over me. I relaxed with that thought and then thought, *This is absolutely amazing.* However, this wasn't a new idea but an old one that was taken down from the shelf and dusted off.

I thought, *Hey, if I am heading for financial difficulty, God is already there. If I am heading into a sickness, Jesus is already there to hold my hand. If I am heading into a situation where I will do a great job, with accolades awaiting, Jesus is there waiting to give me the first high five. Sure the task was accomplished by His Spirit, but nonetheless Jesus is there waiting to give me a fist bump. Amazing.*

Whatever season I am approaching, Jesus is already there, so I just need to allow His Spirit to move in me and guide me to Him. What an invigorating thought! I am learning more and more that God has my back. "For it is God that works in you to will and act according to His good purpose" (Philippians 2:13 NIV). I am slowly recognizing this truth. My role in this great adventure is to seek this truth and to allow it. I must not fight it by being fearful or anxious, because I know two things: Jesus is already there, and our team wins every time. "No, in all these things we are more than conquerors through Him who loved us" (Romans 8:37 NIV).

So, if you are facing uncertainty in your not-too-distant future, remember that Jesus is already there to encourage you, to hold your hand, or to say, "Well done, my good and faithful servant, well done. Keep up the good work."

Whatever happens, we know that God holds the future, and so worrying about stuff that hasn't happened does no good. The great thing about having a relationship with Christ is that we know who holds the future, and He is the one who holds our hand.

"May the God of hope [for today and for the future] fill you with all joy and peace as you trust in him, so that you may overflow with hope by the power of the Holy Spirit" (Romans 15:13 NIV, brackets mine).

Press on...

Baby, It's Cold Outside

> For all my wanting, I don't have anyone but You
> in heaven. There is nothing on earth that I desire
> other than You. I admit how broken I am in body
> and spirit, but God is my strength, and He will be
> mine forever.
>
> —Psalm 73:25–26, The Voice

Thank God for the promise that even though I am broken in body
and spirit He will be my strength and will be mine forever. This
promise is for everyone who calls on the name of the Lord. That
is a pretty cool promise because I have had enough of winter. The
cold weather not only affects our bodies, but even more, it affects
our spirits. More and more people today have SAD, or seasonal
affective disorder, which plays games with their spirits.

As far as our bodies are concerned, we can dress for the cold
if we are fortunate enough to have the proper clothing to battle
the intense weather. But the cold can still break our spirits. We
start telling ourselves that we just need to make it through each
cold snap. That is simply not living up to the full promise that
God is our strength.

The more I practice God's presence, the more I realize that
the weather is secondary. During some days in this cold snap

I haven't even realized how cold it was. That's because I was intensely focused on God. Perhaps I was too distracted to notice the cold. If that is the case, God, please distract me more.

The good news is that we can have victory over the cold. The freezing weather is temporary. God's love is eternal, and the more we love, the warmer we feel, distracting us from the bitter cold. Thank you, God, for warm distractions, and for being my strength, both for my body and my spirit.

Plato once said, "The mind controls the emotions, but the emotions control the actions."

The more we practice God's presence, the more our minds get engaged in the things of God. The more our minds get engaged in the things of God, the more our emotions follow what our minds are thinking. The more our minds are focused on the things of God, the more this shows up in our actions. Thank God that He controls our actions when our minds are centered on Him.

God, thank You that even though my body and my spirit are broken, You are my strength for this day and for every day after. You have the best plan. That makes me all warm!

Press on to internal warmth.

What Are You Thinking About?

Hebrews 11 mentions all the heroes of faith who gave their lives for the cause. We need to think about these heroes—Abraham, Moses, Isaiah, and the rest. It is mind-boggling to consider that we are surrounded by all of those people and that they surround us as witnesses to faith. On the one hand this makes me feel insecure, and on the other hand it makes me feel honored and empowered to be on the same team as them. Wow!

After the great discussion of faith found in chapter 11, we read, "Therefore since we are surrounded by such a great cloud of witnesses let us throw off everything that hinders and the sin that so easily entangles. And let us run with perseverance the race marked out for us, fixing our eyes on Jesus, the pioneer and perfecter of faith" (Hebrews 12:1–2 NIV).

This passage helps me to think of my faith life as an endurance race although most of the time I have treated it like a short sprint. Why do we do that? I think it's because we live in a short-term society. We demand that everything be quick and immediate, and we seem to have little appreciation for waiting to see what God will do. That requires patience, which is in short supply today. We are conditioned by society to want everything now. We need to return to another form of conditioning, one that will help us to persevere and to run the race that God has laid before us. We can do this by focusing on Jesus and on His plan for us. Since we are surrounded by such a great ensemble of people cheering us on, what do we have to lose?

Why not start running that race today? That is what I intend to do. I intend to intensify my godly training. Help me, God, to do this as I live in the world, making a difference for You. I want to be bold for You and not tread lightly due to fear. I will go where You want me to go with the cloud of witnesses cheering me on. I choose to think about the heroes of faith. My thoughts are a part of practicing God's presence, and I can control them. I choose to think about the things from above.

I could choose to think about a different group of things. The choice is up to me. I could choose to think about whatever is stressful, like cold winter weather. I could think about whatever is ignoble, dishonorable, unworthy, shameful, contemptible, despicable, and plain mean. I could think about things that aren't pure, lovely, or admirable, things that are not excellent or worthy of praise. Don't think about taking on tasks that you will perform haphazardly. Whatever you do, first choose a different kind of a list. Try this:

"Finally, brothers and sisters, whatever is true, whatever is noble, whatever is right, whatever is pure, whatever is lovely, whatever is admirable—if anything is excellent or praiseworthy— think about such things" (Philippians 4:8 NIV).

I know this doesn't change the fact that it is freezing out (I am writing this during winter in Canada) and that we are in a "polar vortex," a fancy way of saying that it's extremely cold outside. Though the cold may bring us down, let's think about other things. Some people may try to trick us into thinking it's not that cold, telling us to close our eyes and pretend that we are on some tropical island. The problem with this therapy is that we wake up and go outside and quickly learn that it's still cold out. We can trick our minds only for so long.

The best approach to these issues is to think on the things that Paul tells us to consider. When we focus on something for an extended time, we change our mental state. Even though the temperature may be low, our internal temperatures can tell a different story.

When the Son shines internally, He helps us to deal with the external so it doesn't have the same effect on us. Our minds are weak and affected fairly easily by the external. However, when we practice God's presence and think on eternal things, which are true, noble, right, pure, lovely, admirable, excellent, and praiseworthy, our internal temperatures rise, even during a polar vortex. So if the weather is getting you down, start contemplating those things. By so doing, you will be practicing God's presence and changing your internal thermometer.

Press on (even in the polar vortex).

I'm Accepted

For His Holy Spirit speaks to us deep in our hearts
and tells us that we are God's children.
—Romans 8:16 NLT

That is acceptance at its finest!

This morning I was awakened with a song from the eighties. If you know me, you know that isn't so weird, but what was weird was that this was a song by a Christian rock band formed in the late seventies called Degarmo and Key. I hadn't heard that song in many years, but the lyrics started popping into my head. That is how it goes with music. You may not hear a song for twenty years, but then you get some kind of a trigger, you receive retrieval cues from your brain, and suddenly you are transported back in time to when that song was popular. Music is our time machine. The song was called "I'm Accepted."

The song's main message is that I am accepted by the one who matters most, God. I have been thinking about this for some time now.

To be accepted is one of the needs that we all have as people. We all want to be accepted for who we are. But what happens when we aren't accepted for who we are? We try to change ourselves to be someone we aren't. Then we get into all kinds of trouble. If God accepts me as I am, why can't I accept myself? Why do I always strive to be someone else?

Happiness is found in acceptance. I finally learned this lesson. It was only recently, but better late than never, right? By accepting who I am, by accepting my lot in life, by accepting my skills and talents and using them, by accepting love from above, I now know I am who I am supposed to be, and that is living in a state of perfection. This is not perfect in practice but perfect in purpose. If we can learn that for just one day, then we can learn it for two. I am striving to be the best I can be with a balanced approach to life. If I can achieve that for one day, I can do it for two. If two, then three. Before I know it, I will be living in a perpetual state of happiness as a result of my acceptedness.

Accepting myself has another cool effect. I also get to accept others and to appreciate them for who they are. I don't need to worry about changing other people. That is not up to me. My role is to accept people and to spread love and peace. I'm accepted by the one who matters most. Now I will share some of that acceptance, peace, and love. Being accepted is critical if you wish to create a deep, intimate relationship with God. He wants to be in that same relationship because He accepts you first. Having established that relationship, you can enter into intimacy.

Press on...

The Garden Path

As I awoke yesterday morning, I had a tune in my heart and it was a garden song. I think it is called "I Come to the Garden." It got me thinking about a deep relationship with Jesus. I envisioned myself entering a quiet garden in the early morning. I walk around this place of serenity and notice roses growing, and on the roses is some dew, which is why I figure it is early morning. I stop and smell a rose. It has a beautiful fragrance. I quiet my heart and listen. I hear Jesus talking to me. It is an amazing morning. Jesus tells me that He is in the garden with me, walking around and talking. He tells me something very special—that I belong to Him. We linger a little longer in the garden, and I feel great joy at meeting with Jesus, joy I have never known before. It is a great thing to be in the presence of God and to quiet my heart enough to hear Him.

I then notice something else: the birds are not singing. They also have quieted their voices because they recognized the sweet voice of their Creator and also listened quietly. The melody lingered in my heart for a long time, and in my heart there still rings heaven's harmony. The voice of Jesus is so sweet in the quiet of the garden that I want to visit it every morning. So why don't I? Why do I allow myself to get so distracted that I miss out on such a blessing? Jesus is willing to meet me in the garden if I will just deny myself long enough, set aside time, and visit Him.

When I get there, I long to stay, but then I hear Him telling me that He has plans for me and that I cannot stay in the garden all day every day. He says He wants me to do things for Him in my everyday life. He wants me to take those melodies that are ringing in my heart to my workplace, to the gym, and everywhere else I go. Reluctantly I leave the garden and get on with my day. However, as the day continues, I notice that something neat has happened. Jesus is walking ahead of me, preparing the path that He wants me to take. Thank You, Jesus, for meeting with me. I give You this day, and when the day is done, I pray that we will meet again in the still of the night. I also pray that I will stay connected with You throughout my day. Even if it is a bad day by my definition, I pray that I will remember the garden and once again hear Your sweet voice ringing in my ears. Thank You for always being available to meet with me. On my busy days, please send me a gentle reminder to meet You in the garden. Thank You for the garden experience.

Your garden may be a place with flowers that you can stop and smell, or it may be a walking trail that takes you through quiet woods. It may be a place by a river or a brook where you can hear the mesmerizing sounds of the water. One of my favorite garden places is not a garden at all. It is beside the ocean and is especially enchanting early in the morning when I am by myself. For me, this is one of the most spectacular places to be in God's presence. I love it, particularly on a windy day when the waves are roaring and the salt sea splashes up in my face. It is then that I feel God's presence. Wherever your garden may be, set aside time and go there, and when you arrive, take in the sweet presence of Jesus.

Press on...

A Childlike Faith

As I was thinking about the intimacy issue, I was reminded of a story from more than a decade ago. Perhaps I was given this reminder to help me understand faith as a child experiences it. This story dates from a time when my kids were little. (Seems unlikely if you look at them now, but they were once little gaffers) The same thing happened to both of my boys on different occasions.

The two boys liked to explore, especially in malls. Whenever I took them to a mall, they became young explorers looking for a new land to conquer, or at least a new toy. So I made it into a game. I would wait until they took off and follow them at a distance to see what would happen. Because the same thing occurred with both boys at different times, though years apart, I remember it well.

We were in the mall one day, and sure enough, it was exploration time. This was a long trek. My son made a couple of laps made around the mall in seemingly aimless patterns. At least that is what I thought. He would stop from time to time to check out something that caught his eye. Then it happened. I remember my son stopping in the entrance to a store, picking up a toy, and acting like he had just discovered penicillin. Without missing a beat, he said, "Look, Daddy." When he noticed I wasn't there, he panicked. I ran up to him and asked, "What do you have there?" *What a curious thing,* I thought. He walked around the mall all that time, thinking I was there with him somewhere, somehow, and he behaved as such. When he thought I wasn't there, terror set in.

That is the faith of a child. Kids tend to think like that. They seem unaware that a parent isn't with them when they first wander off. In their minds they are off on an adventure, and somehow dad is there with them. My son instinctively thought I would be there when he wanted to show me something. Was that learned behavior, instinct, the faith of a child, or perhaps a mix of all three? I see a parallel with how God loves us and how we should treat Him. We should treat Him like the parent who is always there, because He is.

God is always with us, and we shouldn't be too surprised by that. When we are feeling down, He is there to cheer us up. When we are happy and things are going well, He is there to offer us a high five. When we are lost in a mall or anywhere else, He is there with us, waiting for us to say, "Look, Daddy," and draw Him into our world. He promised us He would never leave us or forsake us, and He will be with us always, even to the end of the age. This idea seems to be hardwired into kids, but we tend to get suspicious of this truth as we grow older and are beaten down by life. We may do things that draw us away from God and make us think, *God would never be near me now, not after I ...*

That is a trick. In fact, God is closer to us than breathing, and that's pretty close. The Bible says we need to come closer to God by seeking His presence. Then He will in turn come closer to us. The funny thing is that God never leaves us. It is we who walk out on God. It is we who break up with Him. The great thing is that God's grace says, "Yes, please come back to Me. I want you back. I can restore you. I can make you even better. Draw near to Me, and I will draw near to you." God wants that intimate relationship with us even more than we want it with Him. He wants us to have that childlike faith.

God desperately wants us to be searching for Him and saying, "Look, Daddy."

Press on...

DEEP SPIRITUAL THOUGHT #516

Mirror, Mirror

> Now all of us, with our faces unveiled, reflect the
> glory of the Lord as if we are mirrors; and so we are
> being transformed, metamorphosed, into His same
> image from one radiance of glory to another, just as
> the Spirit of the Lord accomplishes it.
> —2 Corinthians 3:18, The Voice

Did you ever wake up in the morning and hear the "Hallelujah
Chorus" playing in your mind because you just got a great insight?
This happened for me on January 29, 2013, day seventeen of my
365-day experiment in getting intimate with God. It is fair to
say that guys have a harder time with relationships and perhaps
expressing our feelings. Even the thought of expressing my
feelings sometimes makes me want to puke. Why is that? Simply
put, intimacy takes a lot of work, and we aren't taught that as guys
when we are growing up. At least when I was growing up that was
the case. Guys were supposed to be tough; feelings were for girls.

That is the backdrop to what I am discovering about intimacy
with God. I am now going to reveal the secret to all relationships.
Some of you will probably say, "Duh! Of course that is the secret."
Others may say, "Let me think about that for a while." Still others
may say, "I get it, but it is easier said than done." That is exactly

why this intimacy thing takes time spent alone with God, time in His Word, and time reflecting on His Word and listening to what He has to say to us when we are "in the garden."

The secret to all our earthly relationships lies in the strength of our heavenly relationship. How intimate we are with each other will be directly proportional to how intimate we are with God. The two things are mirror images. As the Scripture passage above says, we reflect the glory of the Lord as if we are mirrors. Our relationship with God becomes a mirror image of all of our other relationships. Are we having problems being intimate with someone? Then we probably have a problem being intimate with God. Are we not always honest with people? Then we probably struggle with being completely honest with God.

I was once sitting in a small group, and the leader asked us to close our eyes and have a quiet moment with God. This was supposed to quiet our hearts so we would be more in tune with what was going on. When the leader asked what I had experienced in that quiet time with God, my answer surprised even me. I didn't say I felt closer to God, I was drawn into His presence, I heard angels singing, or other such responses. Instead I was honest. I simply said I had a hard time having quiet time with God on command. That doesn't work for me. This led other people to share similar thoughts, and the responses became the basis of a great conversation in which we all were drawn closer to God. This resulted from honesty, one of the keys to any healthy relationship, whether with God or with others. A foundation of honesty will lead to many other good things. The more honest we are with God, the more honest we become with others.

If we are experiencing fractured or broken relationships with certain people, we probably need some work with God in a brutally honest, introspective way. Our relationships with people are a mirror image of our relationship with God.

I am sure we have all heard this before, and I have too, many times. The difference for me now is that I am taking the necessary time with God to soak in His presence and to cultivate a right relationship with Him. I have learned that this concept of relational mirror imaging is true. Perhaps I have invented a new term, relational mirror imaging, or RMI for short. In any case our relationship with God is a perfect gauge of how we are doing in relationships with our partners, our families, our friends, and our coworkers.

The key once again is getting yourself in an ever-increasing intimate relationship with God. This shared intimacy with God will help you in all of your other relationships. I cannot stress this concept enough! It is an amazing thing to give up control in your relationship with God and to let Him take the lead. You will start feeling less stressed about today and tomorrow. You will feel less fearful and more loved. And love is the bottom line.

The next time you are passing a mirror in a hallway, stop and take time to reflect on what the image looking back at you is portraying. Is it someone who is seeking a more intimate relationship with God and others, or is it someone who is too busy to stop and reflect. And one more thing to remember: it is the Spirit of the Lord who will accomplish a change of attitude in you!

Mirror, mirror on the wall, who is the most intimate one of all?

Press on...

DEEP SPIRITUAL THOUGHT #717

What's Your Position?

When we meet people for the first time, they often ask an interesting question: what do you do? What a vague question! Well, let's see. I sleep, wake up in the morning, eat breakfast, shower, and spend time with God before I go to work. Oh, you meant, what do I do for work? I get it now. You want to know what it is I do to bring money home to support my family, as if that will lead you to some great truth about me. You don't really want to know who I am and what makes me tick. You simply want to know what my position in society is, where I fit in. Apparently my position will tell you a great deal about who I am.

Why do we do this? And yes, we are all guilty, I have caught myself doing this many times. It is a comfortable cop-out, a way to make small talk, much like the weather. However, the question has value if it is a doorway to the deep. If it leads to more questions and finally to who we are, the question has great value.

Here is a question for all of us to answer: what is your position? I have been thinking about that quite a bit lately in regard to prayer and faith. The more I learn about prayer, the more I see that it is all about position. What is my position in relation to the Father? I don't mean physical position, such as whether I am kneeling or stretched out on the floor facedown in front of a holy God as an act of reverence. These are positions of prayer, but I am talking about something much deeper. Position as in dependence. Position as in humility. Position as in you are strong and I am weak. Position as in apart from God I can do nothing. Position as in it is God who allows me to act according to His good purpose. Position as in total surrender. Position as in full submission to the will of the Father. Position as in denial of myself. Position as in taking up my cross daily and following Jesus. Position as in I must walk as Jesus walked. Position as in Jesus meant the words He spoke. Position as in I declare my full and utter dependence on God's grace and mercy. Position as in here I am; send me. Position as in You are God, and I am human. What is my position?

Prayer gives us the opportunity to assume the right position with God. I want to be so in tune with God that I can come to Him in prayer and assume my position. When we finally understand that we are human and that we desperately need God, our position in coming to Him in prayer changes. We tend to catch ourselves more quickly when we are out of position. Sometimes when we pray, we come to God half-heartedly, thinking in the back of our minds that we are in control. *It would be nice if You helped out in this area*, God, we think, *but if not, I've got it.* We are survivors. We are tough. We are strong-willed. Society has taught us that we can fend for ourselves. We don't need anyone else. We are strong. That is what society teaches us and what we learn on our own as we develop our independence. It is okay to be tough and strong, but when we approach God with this attitude, our prayers take on a whole different meaning. We come to Him for help, as if he were our personal assistant rather than our sovereign Lord. God, could You take care of this, that, and the other thing and heal Aunt Martha's toe? And if You get a chance, could You stop by and pick up my dry cleaning? Oh yeah, I almost forgot. Let's get that world peace thing stepped up a notch. Thanks, God.

I know we don't intend to treat God like that, but we don't spend enough time thinking about who He is. Then we get busy, and the shopping list of prayers comes out. God wants so much more from us than that. He wants intimate conversation. He wants first place in our lives, not leftovers. God wants us to be totally dependent on Him so He has room to maneuver, so He can step in and be our healer, our comforter, our financial provider, our all in all. We just need to get into position.

When we assume the right position in prayer, the effect carries over into our everyday lives, and we become more and more like Jesus. We start to see people as He saw them. The eyes of our hearts are opened, and we begin to live in submission to the will of the Father. We get to know the Father better, and our conversations deepen.

It was said of the famed nineteenth-century preacher Charles H. Spurgeon that he would go from laughing out loud to the position of prayer with the natural ease of one who lived in both realms. He could make a seamless transition. For him, prayer was effortless. He didn't need to prepare his heart, because his heart was always in the right position. Spurgeon's life was not divided into compartments, the one shut off from the other so tightly that all intercommunication ceased. He lived in constant fellowship with his Father in heaven. He was ever in touch with God, and as a result it was as natural for him to pray as it was for him to breathe.

That is the position that I want and strive for. What is your position?

Press on...

DEEP SPIRITUAL THOUGHT #245

What Are You Bragging About?

This morning a passage from Scripture got me thinking. I was struck by some words from Paul as I was reading Galatians. They led me to reflect on our society, the stuff we talk about, and more important what we brag about.

We brag about a lot of stuff. We brag about our sports teams (when they are doing well), we brag about our stuff, and we brag about our accomplishments. I work in an environment where people are coming and going all the time. There are always several conversations taking place at once. People are constantly talking in the lounges, whether they be in the sales area, the members area, or check-in. (I work at a resort.) I wanted to listen a little more intently today and see what I could learn as it relates to the Scripture passage I have been thinking about lately.

I learned a couple of things. Apparently there was a big sale on designer shoes at one of the stores in town. From what I could gather, the sale was quite significant because I counted at least ten people who had bought shoes there. They were bragging about the deals they got. This was subtle boasting. They were not bragging simply because they had designer shoes. They were bragging about the skill they showed in buying those shoes at a fraction of the cost. One of the ladies took the maximum advantage, buying twelve pairs (This must have been some sale.)

I don't get the appeal in this, but that is not the point. The point is that these people were bragging about how much money they saved. And after how many pairs of shoes does this still count as saving money? But I wouldn't stand between a woman and a good sale on designer shoes. I also observed that one of my friends had just bought a new Mercedes and was bragging about it on social media and by showing photos. I guess that also is brag-worthy.

I spent an interesting day observing conversations, which perhaps differ according to the work environment. If I were a fireman, I probably wouldn't hear all about designer-shoe sales. But what do people brag about in your environment?

How does this relate to my journey of practicing God's presence and to the cross? Here is the relevant verse.

"As for me, may I never boast about anything except the cross of our Lord Jesus Christ. Because of that cross my interest in this world has been crucified, and the world's interest in me has also died … What counts is whether we have been transformed into a new creation. May God's peace and mercy be upon all who live by this principle; they are the new people of God" (Galatians 6:14–16 NLT).

The new people of God—I like that. My interest in the world has been crucified, and the world's interest in me has also died. I have been transformed. I am now a part of the new people of God. The new people of God are braggarts. But what are they bragging about? Designer shoes? New cars or other toys?

Nope! The new people of God are bragging about the cross. They are doing this because their interest in this world has been crucified, and the world's interest in them has also died. This happens when we are transformed into the likeness of Christ. We become new creations. This transformation is the central point of the cross—the why behind Christ's death and resurrection. When we are transformed, God's peace and mercy come upon us. When we live by this principle of bragging about the cross and what it accomplished, His peace and mercy overtake us, and we become the new people of God.

The time has come for the new people of God to join forces, to unite in Christ, and to show the world how to live by this new principle of bragging about the cross and its accomplishments. There is nothing wrong with designer shoes, a new Mercedes, or other toys. A problem arises when these things take the place of the cross. When we brag about these things, they have become a part of us, and our interest in them is evident. We must eliminate worldly interests and be transformed into the new people of God. We may be in the world but not of it. I know this can be tricky. The key as always is to keep our eyes on Jesus, the author and perfecter of our faith. We should always keep the cross in the forefront of our minds and never forget that we have been transformed into the new people of God.

The new people of God are braggarts in the cross of Jesus Christ. They are Jesus-driven and not world-driven. They live with God's grace and mercy all over them. Take some time to figure out exactly where you fit and whether you can honestly say that you are a part of the new people of God. That is my prayer for myself and for all who read this. May we together brag about the cross and all its accomplishments, and may we together become and live as the new people of God.

Press on...

DEEP SPIRITUAL THOUGHT #117

An Epidemic of Kindness

As you read this, you may think there isn't much in the way of a deep spiritual thought here, but if you look further you will notice that this reflection is about kindness, one of the fruit of the Spirit. If you are striving for more of that fruit as I am, this thought takes on deeper significance.

With that backdrop, I would like to teach the world to sing in perfect harmony. I'd like to hold it in my arms and keep it company. I'd like to see the world for once all standing hand in hand and hear them echo through the hills for peace throughout the land. Not bad words for a song that started out as "I'd like to buy the world a Coke." This song began as a Coca Cola ad and not vice versa.

In any case, the message is that the world should live in peace and harmony, which is a tall order. Here is an experiment for those who would like to see a little peace and harmony and all things groovy in the land. This is the "I caught ya" experiment. Here is how it works. As you go about your day, look for someone doing something good for someone, saying something nice to someone, or making a kind gesture to someone. Catch someone doing something positive. When you do, tell that person, "Caught ya!" Then say exactly what you caught the person doing. You might say, "Hey, I caught ya. I saw what you did there. You just did such a nice thing for that person."

Let's start calling people out on the good stuff and see what happens. Try this experiment at home, and pay attention to the results.

We may not be able to teach the world to sing in perfect harmony or get people to sit around holding hands in a kumbaya moment. We may not have enough money to buy the world a Coke, but we can all afford to catch people in the act of doing something good and call them out on it. Let's give it a shot. We might make someone's day a little better— not a bad accomplishment. Let's start an epidemic of kindness and see what happens. Who's in?

Press on...

The Great Commission (Check?)

I have been thinking a lot lately about the Great Commission and what it's all about. I have been working in sales for the past eight years, so for me, the great commission has meant I am getting a big paycheck. So here I am, sitting in a coffee shop and writing these words. There are three people at a nearby table, and I had a thought: these people need Jesus. I am not sure why that thought popped into my mind, but it did. I then started to think about witnessing. Why do we witness? Why does the church place such importance on witnessing, or does it today? Is witnessing a thing of the past? Do we talk about it often? Hmm, interesting questions.

The church seemingly used to talk a lot more about witnessing, so much so that I thought it was all about getting the sales numbers up. The game was to see how many destinies could be changed from hell to heaven as a result of witnessing about Jesus. I almost approached this as a sales contest. The pastor might offer incentives. The person bringing in the most converts during the month would win a set of steak knives, and the top witness at the end of the year would win a car—if there was enough revenue tied to the new converts. Now before you condemn me for thinking this way, I know this is not the right way to think about the Great Commission or about witnessing. But what would happen if we did run such a contest?

The problem with this type of thinking is that it is selfish. Look what I can do for Jesus and the kingdom. If I do this for God, He will do such and such for me. Churches that talk about witnessing and evangelism realize that their people know instinctively that they should be witnessing and that they have a good idea why they should be doing it. Sometimes, however, the church's corporate mission statement is driving them, and that isn't enough. To say that we believe in the Great Commission and that every believer should be promoting it isn't compelling enough for most people. Most people need a reason beyond carrying out a mission statement.

How many Christians witness just because they think it is the right thing to do? I don't know, but I have a feeling some people do it out of guilt. I also believe there is another group of people who witness because they are competitive and want to bring in more converts than others do. Other people say, "I just don't feel it, and I want to be genuine in my faith, so I will wait until I am prompted to witness before I talk about Jesus. I will wait until the Holy Spirit lines up the opportunity perfectly and there is no mistaking that I should talk to a person about Jesus." Still other Christians are struggling to get by in their faith, and witnessing would be too much of a stretch for them. *People don't really want what I have anyway,* they tell themselves. Some others that couldn't care less about the Great Commission.

God made evident to me this morning the reason witnessing is important. The best reason to witness is because in our hearts we believe that other people would be better off with Jesus in their lives. We want other people to feel and to think how we feel and think about God. When our hearts experience the love of Christ, which is too great to fully understand, we want others to share that experience. Christ's love fills us to overflowing so that we want to be like Christ, and we want other people to have that love. That is the real reason to witness.

How do we get on board with this plan? One way is to fix our eyes on Jesus, the author and perfecter of our faith. When we are fixated on Jesus, we experience His love in our hearts. Then, out of the overflow of our hearts, our mouths speak. And that is the reason many people witness and are at times a little overzealous. They have met Jesus, and He has changed their hearts. They want family members and friends to experience Christ's love, which leads to the fullness of life. That is why we should share our faith with others.

"Therefore, since we are surrounded by such a great cloud of witnesses, let us throw off everything that hinders and the sin that so easily entangles. And let us run with perseverance the race marked out for us, fixing our eyes on Jesus, the pioneer and perfecter of our faith. For the joy set before him he endured the cross, scorning its shame, and sat down at the right hand of the throne of God" (Hebrews 12:1–2 NIV).

Let's always remember to "consider him who endured such opposition from sinners, so that you will not grow weary and lose heart" (Hebrews 12:3 NIV).

Let us consider Jesus and our own witness, and let us preach the gospel at all times. If necessary, let us use words. Let us remember that Jesus commanded us to be witnesses.

Press on...

Think Tank

Have you ever thought about what you are thinking about? I know that sounds a little complicated, but think about it. What am I thinking about throughout my day? If we were to make every thought obedient to Christ, what would that look like? When I do this exercise I find myself thinking about work, finances, health, family pressures, appointments, groceries, and bills. As I think about these things, stress starts to kick in. So why do I allow myself to think about these things? I know the formula of taking every thought captive, but still I find myself struggling. I think about and then dwell on immediate and long-range problems. When I get like this, I have a choice. I can continue to focus on my problems, or I can take my thoughts captive and make them obedient to Christ, concentrating on the promises found in God's Word. I must then think about those promises rather than about my problems.

I first need to search the Bible to find the life-giving verses that are appropriate to battle the thoughts and the problems I am struggling with. The Bible tells us to think about whatever is good and pure. Our problems certainly aren't good or pure. God can cause good to come about as a result, but we must take those thoughts captive and make them obedient to Christ.

Why do we focus on our problems when we know that this is not beneficial to us? I think this is because we learn from a young age to pay attention to problems. It is natural to worry about them. We learn this from watching our parents and other adults. It is so much easier to worry about our problems than to say, "My problem is this, but the promise I found in God's Word says the opposite." We need to do this enough times to break the ugly pattern that we learned at an early age. We will not get a sense of abundant life until we have broken this pattern. Once we do, we will begin to sense love, joy, peace, patience, kindness, gentleness, goodness, faithfulness, and self-control.

To gain fullness of life, we must stop focusing on problems. Instead of saying, "I don't have enough money for all my needs this month," we should focus on God's promise that we needn't worry about this. "I've got you covered," He tells us. "In fact, I will supply all your needs according to My glorious riches in Christ Jesus if you will just believe the promise over the problem." This is a matter of choice and belief. I have sometimes found myself believing the promise but not wholeheartedly. I believe with my mind, but my heart at times seems not to get the message. I reminded of the man who told Jesus, "I believe, but help me in my unbelief." Jesus didn't say, "It's impossible to have unbelief and belief at the same time." Instead He said that unbelief comes from a hardened heart. The exchange takes place in Mark 9. The disciples were trying to drive out a demon but couldn't because of their unbelief. They had great faith in Jesus, but their unbelief kept them from performing the miracle.

So where does this unbelief come from? From putting focus on the problem rather than looking at the promise. When I do this, I get into trouble. When I focus on the problem, the promise leaves my mind. Then my heart becomes hardened and I am left having to deal with the problem on my own.

It is time to "take every thought captive to make it obedient to Christ" (2 Corinthians 10:5 NIV).

And remember this: "Finally brothers and sisters, whatever is right, whatever is pure, whatever is lovely, whatever is admirable—if anything is excellent or praiseworthy—think about such things" (Philippians 4:8 NIV).

What are you thinking about?

Press on...

DEEP SPIRITUAL THOUGHT #367

Problem vs. Promise: The Main Event

Does God have a sense of humor? I can assure you He does. As I was praying about trusting the promise more than the problem, an interesting thing happened. For every problem I encounter I have realized there is a promise that trumps it. I was driving around praying one morning, and I had an interesting discussion with God about this issue. I said, "God, I get the fact that I have to trust the promise more than the problem, and I know I sometimes have unbelief even though I believe. Forgive me for my unbelief and help me to do better. I know this happens as a result of a hardened heart, so please soften my heart." Then I prayed, asking, "How do I do this? How do I focus on the promise over the problem? What is the formula? Is there some percentage involved? Should I solve a problem on my own up to a certain point, doing what I can do, and then let the Holy Spirit take over? How does it work? God, what percentage am I responsible for?"

I was getting frustrated, and just at that point I passed an electronic sign in front of a ski shop. It was flashing the message "40 percent," probably for some kind of sale. My mood changed immediately and I started to laugh. I probably would have been rolling on the floor if I hadn't been driving. "Good one, God," I said. "You really got me on that one." God really does have a sense of humor. I still laugh about His prank.

Immediately I understood that there are no percentage formulas. Well, actually there is: I need to focus on Him 100 percent of the time, and He will work in and through me 100 percent of that time. There is a promise for every problem that I encounter, and if I trust God, He will show me the solution. Then I have to act in obedience.

The morning of my percentage encounter, I was awakened by a song on the radio. (Yes, I still wake up to the radio.) The song was about a promise that tells us, "As scripture says, anyone who believes in him will never be put to shame" (Romans 10:11 NIV).

I quickly jotted this down and reflected on it. This was one of the promises from God's Word that I had been thinking about. *How do I get these promises?* I wondered. The answer was by reading and listening, and the message was on the radio. My first spiritual thought of the day involved a promise. The promise was that anyone who trusts in God will never be put to shame. This Scripture verse was addressed to the Jews and the Gentiles, telling them that God doesn't play favorites. He is looking for people who will trust Him wholeheartedly and who will focus on His promises. These people will never be put to shame. That one word *anyone* tells us a lot about God. It includes many types of people.

God gives generously to anyone who calls upon Him. His is an over-and-above type of giving. This is not the prosperity gospel type of giving that makes us rich when we trust in God, but the type of giving that makes us complete and allows us to enjoy the fullness of life. We must do our part by trusting and obeying. We must accept the promise as real and say, "Yes, it applies to me. God said it in His Word, so if it's in His Word it must be true. If it must be true and I am a believer, then it is true for me. So that promise is for me, and I accept it as truth." This total abandonment will send our problems packing.

We are so used to trusting ourselves due to our self-sufficiency that it is difficult to make the switch to total abandonment, but that is what we must do. I have learned, however, that it is possible to have unbelief but still believe. Faith with unbelief says I accept that God is able to do this or that or I know God can do this in general, but I am not sure if it will happen for me. This is faith with unbelief.

Faith with belief says that because God is able to do this or that, He will do it for me. It is a promise in His Word. He spoke it to me in a promise, so my problem can be cast aside.

Accepting "God will" over "God can" brings total abandonment in belief. That bridge is tough to cross for many of us who have learned to be self-sufficient and not to talk about our problems or ask anyone for help, believing we are in control.

We must change this attitude. We need to be aware that faith with unbelief is possible but that we can also choose fullness of life and faith with belief. The choice is up to us. What do you choose?

God promises us that He will supply all our needs, that His grace is sufficient for us, providing an escape from temptation, that all things work together for the good of those who love Him, and that if we believe in Jesus we will be saved. He has even promised resurrection from death, which comes with eternal life. Those are some cool promises that I choose to accept.

Press on...

DEEP SPIRITUAL THOUGHT #223

Faith

It is day fifty-four of my 365-day experiment with drawing near to God. Today I have been thinking about Christ's words on faith, specifically about faith and a little seed. He seemed to be talking directly to me. The conversation might go something like this.

"Oh, Trevor, you have so little faith. You talk a big game, but when it comes right down to it, where is your faith? If you had faith the size of a little mustard seed, you could say to Blue Mountain (Collingwood, Ontario), 'Pick yourself up and jump into Georgian Bay,' and the mountain would listen to you."

"What do You mean by that, Jesus? Is the mountain representative of my problems? Does it represent my finances, my biggest fears about life, health, or other areas where I struggle with faith? Or can I really tell the mountain to throw itself into the lake and it will listen to me?"

After pondering this for a bit, I concluded that God doesn't want me moving His furniture around. (The earth is, after all, His footstool.) So I decided the mountain must be representative of something else.

Jesus is saying to me that if I believe even a little bit, everything changes. The more I believe in His promises, the more stuff changes. Even the biggest of my problems can be overcome with a little bit of faith in a promise.

Something to think about: "And without faith it is impossible to please God" (Hebrews 11:6 NIV). Faith is a gift from God. What am I doing with this gift?

Jesus mentions this mustard-seed faith twice in the New Testament. In Matthew 17:14–20, the disciples were unable to drive a demon from a young boy even though Jesus had given them authority to do it. He said their lack of faith made it impossible for them to do this. Then He used the mountain analogy. With mustard-seed faith, nothing will be impossible for you.

Jesus told His disciples: "If you have faith as small as a mustard seed you can say to this mulberry tree, be uprooted and planted in the sea, and it will obey you" (Luke 17:6 NIV). In using the example of this tiny seed (one of the smallest), Jesus was speaking figuratively about the incalculable power of God when unleashed in the lives of those with faith. He was using hyperbole to make a point.

The parable of the mustard seed in Matthew 13:31–32 talks about a seed growing into a huge tree, representing the humble beginnings of Christianity. A few disciples preached the gospel, and it spread to the ends of the earth. That is what Jesus calls mustard-seed faith.

Two thousand years later, the gospel has spread from a little area with a few people preaching it and has become a worldwide creed. Only a little bit faith, the size of a mustard seed, is required. Thank God that all it takes is a little faith. Just a little turn of the head toward God could be enough to conquer your problems. With faith all things are possible. The next time you have mustard on a burger or a hot dog or have one of those fancy grainy mustards with other types of meat, remember the seed, remember what Jesus said, and release that faith.

Press on...

Breakthrough Training

Do you want to have a breakthrough with God? Do you want to take your faith up another level? That is what has been happening to me with my promise vs. problem thinking. When I write these insights, they are first permeating my inner mind for days so I that understand more and more of the things of God. When I control my thoughts or think about things that draw me closer to God, I get new ideas in the weirdest places. I may be sitting in a coffee shop or a hot tub or I may be driving around, and a lot of the time these ideas come in the wee hours of the morning when I wake up and start praying. In any case, I had a breakthrough in this promise vs. problem thinking. My faith is increasing and I am becoming more intentional. This prolonged thinking has allowed me to switch my own innermost beliefs from God can to God will. A lot of us remain at the "God can" stage and believe that "God will" for other people but not for us.

Faith is like the muscles I am trying to build at the gym. I work certain muscle groups repeatedly, and eventually I see gains. This takes a lot of dedication and hard work. The same is true with developing my faith. There are disciplines involved such as prayer, spending time with God, and reading His Word. These aren't rocket-science insights but the basics. If we aren't doing the basics, however, these ideas seem advanced. This breakthrough training also brings a shift in reading God's Word. Before I started this 365-day experiment, I read the Word as a book or as separate stories, They could apply to me, but they seemed better suited for others. Now I am reading God's Word and believing it intellectually as well as with my heart. I am intentionally engaging my mind and my heart as I read. This makes all the difference. I am slowly shifting from telling myself, *That stuff in the Bible is for other people*, to thinking, *Wow! That passage was written just for me. Very cool.*

When you purposefully engage in breakthrough training with God, you start to believe what He says in His book and you start living as if it is directly related to you. Fascinating stuff. When you live your life according to God's promises and commands, the switch occurs from God can to God will. Will He answer all your prayers as you want? Come on now. We aren't dealing with a magic vending machine where we insert our prayers and the answer we want comes out. We are dealing with almighty God, who knows a lot better than we do. So sometimes when we make a request, He will answer, "Not likely, but My grace is good enough for you, and I promise it will get you through the obstacle, problem, or issue you are facing. That you can take to the bank."

As you draw closer to God, you understand better what to pray for, and slowly the things you pray for change. I have spent months praying that I would be drawn closer to God, and slowly but surely that prayer is being worked out in my life. Paul encourages us to pray about everything, but the closer we are to God, the more we learn what we should seek.

I believed for the longest time that God could always do stuff for other people. My faith was never shaken in that area. I believed that "God can" with the best of them. So what was holding me back from "God will" for me? My lack of faith was directly related to the fact that I believed God's Word for other people but not for myself. My problems were always more dramatic than other people's, and they were always bigger than God's promises. That is what I unthinkingly assumed. I now choose to believe God's Word for what it is—truth, life, and a road map giving me direction and purpose.

Fear prevents us from taking that leap from God can to God will. Once we eliminate fear, then we have to believe. But we persist in saying, "Yes, I believe God can do this and that for me," but adding, "Only if He wants to, and I am not sure if He does." It is almost as if we place an escape clause in our faith. We believe to an extent but think that God will act only up to a certain point. We create a back door for Him. That is how I behaved for years in my faith. But that is changing as I continue my breakthrough training. Just as I am training my body through different forms of exercise, I am training my faith. I know that God can, but will He? That is the question. The answer is yes. God will make sure His promises come true because they are just that, His promises. So rest assured that if God gives you a promise, He not only can but will keep it.

An old adage comes to mind: God said it; I believe it; that settles it. This is breakthrough faith.

"For all of God's promises have been fulfilled in Christ with a resounding 'Yes!' And through Christ, our 'Amen' (which means 'Yes') ascends to God for his glory" (2 Corinthians 1:20 NLT).

Press on...

DEEP SPIRITUAL THOUGHT #107

The Day the Sun Didn't Come Up

I was awake at 4:30 this morning (which is not abnormal). After an unsuccessful attempt to go back to sleep, I got up at 5:19. I decided to hike to the beach, which is only five minutes away. It was still dark as I was walking around Sunset Point, and I thought, *What if the sun doesn't come up today?* This was a hypothetical question, because we take it for granted that the sun will be up or at least that the sky will brighten. I went for a walk to see the sunrise.

So I was sitting on a park bench watching the sky and wondering what would happen if the sun didn't rise. What if I sat there for hours and hours and then nothing? What if I sat there for the whole day and nothing happened and then it was night again? I would definitely start thinking that the end was near or that something cataclysmic was about to happen. What if I got up the next morning and did the same thing and still no sunrise? This was horrific to think about. It was also horrific to consider that I take such a blessing for granted. *What else do I take for granted?* I wondered.

You know the end of this story. The picture I took at the end of my time at the beach tells a much better tale than I ever could. It shows one of the most beautiful sunrises I have ever seen. Seeing it, I immediately had a new appreciation for the artist who made that painting. When the sun rose this morning it was glorious. My heart skipped a beat and I was thankful. This is what came to mind: The steadfast love of the Lord never ceases. His mercies never come to an end. They are new every morning. Great is Your faithfulness, O God. Thank You for a beautiful sunrise!

Press on...

The Family of God, Adoptions, and Heirs!

How can I relate to God through Jesus? This is the question on my mind. As I was reading Galatians, the thought struck me that God's Word is living and active. The thought arose because I had gone through Galatians the previous month with what I thought was a fine-tooth comb, but I got a different meaning as I was reading one of the same passages.

"But when the right time came, God sent His Son, born of a woman, subject to the law. God sent him to buy freedom for us who were slaves to the law, so that he could adopt us as his very own children. And because we are his children, God has sent the Spirit of his Son into our hearts, prompting us to call out, Abba, Father. Now you are no longer a slave but God's own child. And since you are his child, God has made you his heir" (Galatians 4:4–7 NLT).

These verses tell me that I am a part of a much greater family. I am now adopted as one of God's kids, and the Bible tells me I can even call Him Abba, a much softer version of Father. When I think of our Father in heaven, I think power. He is in heaven and so much greater than all of us. However, His Word tells me that God changed this dynamic when He sent His Son. Jesus bought me freedom from the law and the opportunity to be adopted into

His family. Furthermore, God then placed the spirit of His blood Son in my heart, making it possible for me to cry out the softer Abba, or Dad, or Daddy.

Imagine that. God adopted the likes of me as His son, so I can call Him Dad. Now I can pray with the intimacy of Dad instead of just Father. Dad, I really need help with this issue. Dad, I could sure use some extra cash about now. Dad, I feel sick. Can you help me with that? This changes everything. God sometimes says yes to our requests, sometimes no, and sometimes yes on the condition that we learn a lesson first. God our Father or Dad always has our best interest in mind. Father really does know best. We get to have an intimate relationship with Him. When we commit to a moment-by-moment relationship with Him, He switches from the formal our Father who art in heaven to the familiar Dad.

Since I am His child, He has made me an heir. I am a joint heir with Jesus. The fact that I am God's heir should allow me to trust Him fully for everything and in every situation. The almighty God of creation is adopting me as His child and making me an heir to the kingdom. Wow! That is a promise definitely worth noting.

What if we all understood what it meant to be the family of God? Would we treat our fellow believers differently if we understood they were our brothers and sisters? Wouldn't it be exciting to start living this out in the church and to show the world this great love? I want to be a part of a vibrant family of God. Let's do it!

Press on...

Am I Enough?

What a rough day yesterday was. I spent a full day yelling at God, begging Him to change my situation. It was day seventy of my 365-day experiment, and I had experienced much spiritual growth. I was on the verge of yet another spiritual breakthrough, so the circumstances were intensified. Instead of praying for God to change my situation, I should have been praying for Him to change my approach and to show me where I needed to change. I had years of experience with begging God to change my situation and would end up getting frustrated with Him because I couldn't see His power at work in my life. I used to get so frustrated with this that I would eventually stop trying and stop praying.

I realize this was an adolescent approach to prayer and faith, but when you are in the middle of a tantrum over God, it is hard to see anything. Instead of ranting, the approach I needed to take was to relax and to focus on the intimacy of my relationship with God. Intimacy sometimes involves heated arguments, but this argument was one-sided. I was yelling at God when I should have been listening. I realized that I needed to know God and to be known by Him. I needed to draw near to God so He could draw near to me. I needed to resist the Devil so he would flee from me and to submit myself to the authority of Christ. That is the formula that I needed to practice on the day of the great rant, but I chose a different approach.

For seventy days, I had been trying to be more intimate with God, but instead of continuing on that path, I figured yelling and screaming at Him to change my situation would somehow make me feel better. So there I was, yelling at God, pleading with Him to show me a miracle, demanding to see signs and wonders and spiritual power to improve my situation. I was like a raving lunatic. God must have been laughing at His spoiled child. Then again, He may have been thinking, *How dare he? What gives him the right to yell at Me?* Luckily God's grace covers my sins and stupidity. My yelling and screaming were accompanied by weeping and wailing, and maybe even gnashing of teeth. Then the yelling and screaming turned to sighs. Finally I was quiet. I was like a baby who had just cried himself to sleep. Babies are intense for a while, and then they finally calm down. That is what I was like on the morning of day seventy.

After quieting my mind and my soul, I heard from God. This was as real an experience as I have ever had with God. He wasn't yelling and screaming at me. Instead I heard a quiet voice. I will never forget this. Only three words were spoken, but another thousand were implied.

Am I enough?

It was as if all the work I had been doing for the past seventy days was being spoken back to me. The whole idea of this experiment was to have an intimate relationship with God. Now He was asking, "Am I enough? I thought more than anything you wanted an intimate relationship with Me and didn't care much about the things I could give you. I thought you wanted to get to know Me more. Is knowing Me good enough? If you never receive any of these things that you are praying for but know Me well, is that enough? What if you do not see all these signs and

wonders and miracles and outpourings of spiritual power? Am I
enough? Is an intimate relationship with Me enough?"

That was a humbling experience, and you would think there
was an obvious answer to this question. Well, think again. My
initial response was, "No, God. That is not enough." I know what
you are thinking: are you out of your mind? I did say that was my
initial reaction. However, when I thought about it for a while, I
came to an overwhelming conclusion. "Yes, God," I said. "You
are enough for me. If I never see another miracle, healing, sign,
wonder, or outpouring of Your Holy Spirit, that is all right. I am
content to sit at the feet of Jesus and soak in His presence. I am not
very good at it, but so help me God, that is more than enough."
I finally realized after twenty-five-plus years of adhering to the
Christian faith that I was focusing more on the effect than the
cause. What God's power could do for me was somehow more
appealing than Jesus Himself. I realized I had completely missed
the point. If degrees were awarded for missing the point, I would
have a Ph.D.

Understanding this and being content with that intimacy
will help with all my other relationships. We were created for
relationships. Having an intimate relationship with God affects
all of our other relationships so that we slowly become who we
are supposed to be. And that is someone designed to love and to
be loved. This shared intimacy with God becomes the benchmark
for every successful relationship.

The whole point is to seek God first. Then other relationships
will be healthy. Wait a minute. Seek God first. That reminds me
of something.

Instead of ranting and raving about wanting stuff, "Seek the
Kingdom of God above all else, and live righteously, and he will
give you everything you need" (Matthew 6:33 NLT).

Press on, (And just for the record, God is enough!)

The Counselor

Do you ever wonder what Jesus would look like if He were here today? If Jesus burst into our time, how would that look? I recently saw a picture of Jesus sitting on a park bench, talking to a young man. The man was wearing clothes of this era, but Jesus was dressed in a white robe. The artist probably intended to differentiate Him and make Him stand out. Looking a little more closely, I noticed how the two were sitting. Jesus was sitting a little sideways with an arm outstretched and His hand resting on top of the bench's back. Based on His body language, He was in the position of authority. The young man was sitting slightly bent over with his elbows resting on his knees and his hands on his face. His body language showed that he was the one getting advice, and Jesus was giving it.

This picture painted a thousand words. I was reminded of Christ's promise that He would send His counselor to be with us always. I pictured myself as the young man on the park bench asking advice from Jesus and having a conversation with Him. The picture was a great reminder that Jesus has made it possible for me to have this direct counsel. In fact, He goes to God on my behalf and intercedes for me. This got me thinking about the roles of God, Jesus, and the Holy Spirit in history and in my life.

Before God had asked me, "Am I enough?," I would continually pray for the Holy Spirit to be evidenced in power. I read in God's Word about the resurrection power that is available to me, about all the miracles God performed in the Old Testament times, and about the miracles Jesus did in the New Testament era, and I would pray to experience that type of power. Until God set me straight with knowledge of Himself, that was how I would pray. I still think it is good to pray this way but not to be consumed by it. When we become consumed by this type of prayer, we focus on the results and not on the person. When we focus on God, these things will happen as God intends. That is why we need to be mindful when we pray. When we pray for God's will on earth as in heaven, we must buy into God's plan for us rather than our idea of this plan. This changed my thinking about how God, Jesus, and the Holy Spirit interact with us. Here is what I learned.

God is all-powerful and sometimes deals with us through power and miracles. I sometimes wish that God would interact with me the way He did with people in the Old Testament—perhaps in a burning bush, in a cloud, or by some other dramatic means. Then I think, *Wait a minute. I seem to recall a Scripture verse from the Old Testament saying that no one sees God and lives. That is the God of power that I do not want to see.* I then remember that there were hundreds of years of silence in between miracles in the Old Testament and that change was painfully slow. I started asking a different question. Why do I want to hear God's voice from a burning bush? He intervenes with us in a different way today. In fact, I have concluded that there have been three phases in history and that God has intervened differently in each one. I believe He has done this so that over thousands of years we would see His full character.

In the Old Testament, God chose Moses, used him for a purpose, and followed up with hundreds of years of silence. The prophet Samuel's call came at a time where God rarely spoke and there were few visions. God's pattern during this phase was to perform miracles through a chosen person, wait a long time, and then choose someone else. I feel disappointment because I want to see miraculous displays of God's power, but then I fail to have a burning-bush experience. I need to remember that miracles are only a part of God's character and that His plan involves so much more.

Looking to the New Testament to see how God intervenes, I discover something right away. In the gospels I read about supernatural activity that is changing everything. Jesus is here, and He is changing all the rules. At this point, everyone seeking God went to the temple where He was present in the Holy of Holies. Jesus said that God's presence would be relocated to a rather unlikely place—us, ordinary people like you and me. Our bodies would become God's temples, and Jesus said that believers would worship in spirit and in truth and not just in places made by hand. Jesus also performed many miracles, not as a global panacea but as signs pointing people toward God.

Jesus came to repair the broken relationship between us and God. We would no longer have to approach God through a priest with sacrifices, because through His shed blood, Jesus offered the ultimate sacrifice, allowing us direct access to God. We became God's temples; our bodies became the Spirit's home. Through His sacrifice, Jesus has reconciled us to God so that we may once again commune with Him directly. Jesus has become our high priest and our advocate. He prays to God on our behalf.

Jesus made all of this possible with the cross. The cross was the point in history where God chose to take care of the sin issue. In the cross event, God revealed His judgment on sin. This event not only shook the earth and tore the veil in the temple to give us access to God, but it also shook the foundation of hell and changed how evil was allowed to operate from that point on. The cross was the most important event in history. We, the human race, were finally restored to a right relationship with God. This event made it possible for every person ever born to have a relationship with God. Jesus came for that reason, to make us right with God. The cross is the event where God and sinful man meet. God defeats death, and a whole new way of life is opened up.

So let's review. As a general rule, God does not operate through power as He once did. He still offers miracles and signs and wonders, but things have changed. I now know why. The reason is a relationship. Sometimes I wish He would speak to me in a burning bush, smite an occasional enemy, or burn up the enemies' prophets as He did with the prophets of Baal. Then I realize the kingdom no longer advances in that manner. That was phase one, which established whom we were dealing with. In phase two, God showed us another side of Himself and sent His Son so we could be reconciled to Him. He showed us just how much He loved us. At the end of phase two, Jesus sets up phase three and the advancement of the kingdom through grace and freedom. How did He do that?

Jesus set up phase three by telling us we would have access 24/7/365 to our very own counselor, the Spirit of God Himself. And so we have returned to the park bench analogy, with Jesus counseling the young man.

How does a good counselor work? Is it by dictating how we should change and by telling us how shortsighted we are? Absolutely not!

A good counselor works from the inside out. The counselor gets us talking about our feelings, and our innermost secrets and pains are brought to the surface and dealt with. That is how a good counselor works, and that is how phase three works in this spiritual adventure called life. We get to talk to God personally through the work Jesus did and through the promised counselor. Jesus tells us that He must leave in order to advance the kingdom and that we will do more works than He has done because of this promised Spirit. That is God working in us to will and to act according to His good purposes. So we see it all coming together.

In phase one, we had the law, lots of rules, and an all-powerful God.

In phase two, the all-powerful God showed us His all-loving side and sent His Son Jesus to fulfill the law by offering the ultimate sacrifice: His life for our reconciliation.

In phase three, we are given the ultimate comfort, along with advice whenever we need it. We are given the Spirit of God to live in us. God has moved from pillars of clouds by day and pillars of fire by night to living inside of us. His Spirit is now closer than breathing. Words cannot begin to describe a love that great. The only response I can think of to such grace is to fall on my face and say, "Thank You, God. I know I do not deserve this, but thank You. Thank You for showing yourself in history. Thank You for Jesus. Thank You for giving me a comforter and a counselor when Jesus left this world."

"I will ask the Father to send you another helper, the Spirit of truth. The world does not recognize the Spirit of truth, because it does not know the spirit and is unable to receive Him. But you do know the Spirit because He lives with you, and He will dwell in you" (John 14:16–17 The Voice).

Not only do we get our own personal counselor, but He is the spirit of truth. He will never lie to us. He speaks to us gently, and He is enough!

The next time you pass a park bench, sit down, relax, close your eyes, and listen for the counselor. Listen carefully and you will hear that still small voice.

Now may the God of all power, all love, all comfort, and all counsel be your God in ever increasing measure.

Press on...

75

The Seven Habits of Highly Effective Seekers

Is it possible to be in constant contact with God throughout the day? Is it possible to focus my mind that much? My mind seems to wander every few seconds, so is it possible to focus it throughout my day wholly on God? Is it possible to focus on God 24/7? What about distractions? How do I deal with them? Society dictates that I must work to make a living so I can get money to buy stuff, but what happens on the job? Is it possible to incorporate thoughts of God into my workday? Would that create too much of a battle in my mind, causing my work to suffer? Can we focus on God after the workday is done? What happens when the kids need our attention after a long day of work? What about our other relationships? Is it possible to stay connected to that higher power and to live in His presence throughout the day, through all our trials, through our dealings with other people, and with all the other stuff that the world throws at us?

These are great questions. If we could stay focused on God throughout the day and not get sidetracked by life's distractions, it would be a lot easier to keep that connection. However, reality dictates a different set of circumstances. Going out into the world every day is like going down into the mines. I was in a mine deep under the earth and was given a white suit to wear before I entered. White was an interesting choice. When I came out of the mine into the light of day, I noticed that my suit was no longer white. There was dust all over it. I was in an iron ore mine, but that is not as bad as a coal mine. Coal dust is everywhere. When you come out of a coal mine you are covered in it. When we go out into the world, we get the stuff of the world on us. The more of this world dust that we have on us, the more our connection with God gets disrupted. However, the more connected we are with God throughout the day, the less world dust gets on us. So is it possible to stay connected to God throughout the dusty day? This is impossible with man but quite possible with God. In fact, with God all things are possible.

Let's together try an experiment just for one day. Let's focus our minds enough so that we consciously think about God, recall Scripture passages, sing songs to ourselves, and encourage others on the same path. When we have had one successful day of this, let's try two days, then three, and so on. What do you suppose would happen if a few people started living like this? And what would happen if they told two friends, and they told two friends, and so on? Do you suppose this might change the world a little bit? I know we would have less world dust on us. For this to happen, we must undertake some spiritual disciplines, understand our interruptions, and recognize those interruptions so we can effectively deal with them.

I have been thinking about this plan for several months, and I have realized that to pull it off, we need to identify helpful habits and to practice them on a daily basis. I have come up with a top-seven list, or seven habits of highly effective seekers. These are basic, but if they aren't yet part of your life they are advanced.

God speaks to me through His Word. By reading His Word, believing it applies to me, and living according to it, I can drastically reduce the amount of world dust I get on me.

Pray about everything. The word *everything* applies to an awful lot, but that is exactly what God wants us to do. Talk to Him about everything.

Give thanks in all situations. The word *all* takes in a lot of situations. I know this is difficult, but finding a way to be thankful in all situations will keep world dust at a distance. God is amazing at bringing good from painful events. This one is like exercise: the more you do it, the easier it gets. Physical training has value, but godly training has far greater worth.

Get alone with God in nature and appreciate what He has created. Going for walks by yourself in the great outdoors is a good way to focus your mind. It is good for your soul and for getting rid of world dust.

Will yourself to think about God every half hour or so. This can be through Scripture or song. Think about kingdom stuff.

Be quiet! Get alone with God and ask Him to speak to you. This requires focus and practice because our minds tend to wander every few seconds.

Get other believers on board. Working at this with someone else is beneficial, especially when you want to give up. It is also neat to share your results with someone else and to help that person battle world dust. This is like having a workout partner. You can keep each other accountable. A small group of like-minded people also works well.

How much world dust would we get on us if we practiced these habits every day? There's only one way to find out.

A good way to keep track of whether you are developing these habits is to write them down. Record what happened when you spent the whole day focusing your mind or what you learned when you were alone in nature. Record what happens throughout your day when you practice these spiritual disciplines. Doing this could be seen as an eighth habit, or it could be a way of bringing these habits together. In any case ...

"Physical training is good, but training for godliness is much better, promising benefits in this life and in the life to come. This is a trustworthy saying, and everyone should accept it" (1 Timothy 4:8–9 NLT).

Press on...

DEEP SPIRITUAL THOUGHT #129

My Valentine

Valentine's Day is fast approaching, and this has led me into some interesting areas of thought. My first reaction to Valentine's Day is, why do people buy into this contrived holiday and use it as an opportunity to show love once a year? Are they trying to make up for all the times throughout the year when they failed to show love? The day started with the story of St. Valentine, but what have the marketers made of it today? Are the chocolate makers looking to boost sales? (Who needs an excuse to buy chocolates?) Perhaps the flower companies needed a spike in sales before Mother's Day? I don't know, but we as a culture buy into Valentine's Day hook, line, and sinker.

Whatever the reason for Valentine's Day, the only thing that matters is how we handle it each year. It is like every commercialized day throughout the year. Marketers cry for our hard-earned money and get it. People feel obligated to spend lots of money because a well-thought-out ad campaign, coupled with society's acceptance of consumerism, tells them they should. But I am not on a mission to ban these days. That would be fighting the wrong battle. Instead I hope that on this Valentine's Day we start to consider the reasons we are spending money on flowers or chocolate for our loved ones.

I started thinking about this many months ago shortly after God brought a special lady back into my life from my college days twenty-five years ago. Those who know me know I am by no means an expert on relationships. But in a way I am. I have made enough mistakes in relationships to learn how to properly handle one. I have learned in the school of hard knocks. This time around I have changed my approach. I have learned the secret to great relationships. I will explain.

Because of my upcoming marriage, I have been thinking a lot about Jesus' words in Matthew when He quotes Scripture and talks about the two becoming one flesh and about God joining two people together. I decided last year to be content with growing my relationship with God rather than focusing on pursuing relationships with the opposite sex. After I had given up that part of my life to God, He brought the woman who is to become one flesh with me into my life. Immediately after we started dating, God gave me a prayer for the relationship. It was a simple but powerful prayer: God help me to love Trilbi as Christ loved the church.

Christ loved His church so much that He promised that He would build it and that the gates of hell could not stand in opposition. This means that Christ will fight for His church, shed His blood for it, nurture it, and build it up. I thought, *That is a lot of love, in fact too much for me to pull off.* Then it dawned on me. God will love through me. I just need to be sensitive to His Spirit and obedient when called upon. I can love only because He first loved me. That has been my daily prayer, that I would love my future wife, and then my wife, as Christ loved the church. The church is the bride of Christ, which is why that prayer is fitting on so many levels. I certainly don't always meet this mark, but when I feel little or no love, I simply say that prayer and God directs my mind to where it should go. I have discovered the secret to strengthen any relationship: make sure it is committed to God, and be open to love as Christ loved the church. That advice is mostly for men, because the man has the God-given responsibility to love His wife as Christ loved the church. Once that happens, the woman's role will also be a godly one and she will love with a godly love. If you don't believe me, try it for yourself.

A question remained in my mind, however. What does it mean for the two to become one flesh? After much soul searching and months of asking God, I have the foundation for a great answer. Most people think the two become one flesh because they can now have sex in the eyes of the church. Sex certainly is a part of the two becoming one flesh, but there is so much more depth of meaning. There is having sex, and there is becoming one flesh. People can have sex, but are they one flesh? When I was a teenager growing up in Newfoundland, I would hear the term *getting laid* quite often. I am sure everyone reading this has heard the term. It is a crude way of talking about meaningless sex. But most people do not realize that its origins are from the Bible.

The Bible uses at least two words for the act of sex. One is *lay*. So and so lay with so and so. You can read this throughout the Bible. The past tense of *lay* is … *laid*. People get laid in many sexual relationships today. Big deal! The Bible also talks about the two becoming one flesh. The other word for the sexual act is *knew*. Adam knew Eve. The two were one flesh (figuratively and literally since she came from his rib). You become one flesh when you know your wife or your husband. Some will say that this is a stretch, but I think the sexual act and the two becoming one flesh can be related to God's love for us. God loves us intimately, and our earthly relationships are to reflect that love.

The two becoming one flesh has other meanings. Becoming one flesh isn't confined to the flesh. The two also become of one mind. This can happen only when both parties are sold out to God's will and God's way in their marriage and the self agenda takes a back seat. In a relationship, you should be able to ask the other person a simple question: is that thought coming from self or from God? You must be able to give each other a checkup from the neck up without getting angry and upset to see whose agenda is at the forefront. Becoming one mind gets easier the more you know the other person, so spend many hours conversing and getting to know your partner.

The two becoming one flesh also applies emotionally, intellectually, financially, and most important spiritually. What God brings together man dare not separate. When God brings two people together it is a beautiful thing. It is poetry in motion. You know a love that you could never have known on your own. It comes from God and must be nurtured by Him. God is also the keeper of this oneness of flesh. Without God, it is next to impossible to love and to serve your partner as Christ loved and served the church. Spiritual growth individually, as a couple, as a family, and with your local church is vital to continue on the road of oneness. The more you are open to God and are drawing near to Him, the more He is drawing near to you. Help your partner and your family grow in faith.

Taking the marriage vows doesn't mean you automatically become one flesh. That is where God's love comes in. You must pray every day that God will help you love your partner as Christ loved the church. Then you can begin the journey of the two becoming one flesh. That is my prayer as I head into my own marriage. I know many of you may say, "Wait until you are married for a number of years. Then see how you feel." I understand your skepticism, but since I have been taking myself out of the equation and practicing God's presence, I find that He is changing me in every area of my life, and the experience only gets more intense each day. My relationship with Him takes work, but that work makes every other area of my life easier because I am allowing God to work in and through me. My go-to verse for the spiritual discipline of practicing God's presence is this: "For it is God who works in you to will and to act in order to fulfill his good purpose" (Philippians 2:13 NIV).

I not only believe this but live it. God is doing it, and God will do it. To God be the glory.

Now back to the Valentine's Day issue. You don't have to wait until Valentine's Day to declare your love to your partner. I am a very private person and usually would not talk about my personal relationships, but by writing this today, I am declaring in front of many witnesses and God that I will attempt to love Trilbi Jane just as Christ loved the church. That is my Valentine's Day gift to Trilbi. (I know you are thinking, *Cheapskate*.)

I have recently been given another verse that relates to my relationship: "In the same way, husbands ought to love their wives as they love their own bodies. For a man who loves his wife actually shows love for himself" (Ephesians 5:28 NLT).

This verse speaks to me lately because since the first of January I have been paying attention to what I eat and going to the gym quite a bit. I am trying to make my body, which is a temple of the Holy Spirit, into a five-star resort. It had become a cheap hotel because I was not concerned about what I ate or how I treated my body. I was treating it more like a science experiment than the temple that it is, so when I read that verse, it jumped out at me. Before I would have thought, *I don't treat my body very well, so I guess I won't be treating my partner that well either.* That attitude isn't acceptable anymore. The closer I am drawn to God, the more I care about the things that God cares about, and He cares about me and about you. That is why I want to treat my body like the five-star resort that the Holy Spirit deserves. By extension I will treat my partner Trilbi with that same respect.

So Trilbi, instead of giving you expensive gifts on this contrived day for showing affection, I give you my heart and the words that are on my heart. I am thankful that God has brought us together and that He has chosen you for oneness with me. Happy Valentine's Day, Trilbi!

If you are not Trilbi, I hope you can pull some nuggets of truth from this post. May you all love each other more dearly and think through your relationships this Valentine's Day. May you invite God to be the center of each relationship and learn what it means to love with a love that comes from God. Happy Valentine's Day!

Press on...

DEEP SPIRITUAL THOUGHT #328

What Is Your Modem Speed?

Did you ever stop to reflect on why we are so impatient today? If you are not impatient, congratulations. You have learned valuable lessons that should be shared. We want stuff now. We want faster speeds on the Internet, because fast just isn't fast enough. No matter how fast something is, we want it faster. With use search engines because we want answers to our questions without having to spend time thinking things through. Those of us who own digital recorders do not watch television commercials because that would take too much time. We fast forward through all the commercials. We press pause to get a snack. We seem to have everything needed for our convenience. If we watch TV or surf the Internet, we find an incredible amount of information at our disposal. We receive information quickly. With today's technology, our brains never have to slow down. We can turn them on in the morning and subject them to images and information all day long, and when it comes time to shut them down at night we realize it isn't easy. Our brains race from all the images that have entered our conscious and subconscious minds.

So how do we slow our minds and quiet our souls enough to connect with God? With the overload of technology, we have conditioned our minds to be in constant use. I love technology. I love newer, shinier, faster, better, but I also love God. I know that the amount of information I am exposed to makes it harder to connect with Him. I have a hard time connecting with God because I am so distracted by choices online. The only solution for me is scheduling time to meet with Him. There's nothing involving rocket science here, but I need to do it. I then need to make these get-togethers consistent, because it is easy to forfeit my time with God in favor of social media or one of the many programs I have recorded on my PVR. Hey, who watches live TV anymore?

To make matters worse, I have come up with justifiable excuses for not spending time with God. I worked hard all day and need to download (which means sitting in front of the TV and putting more stuff in my mind). I am tired. That is a popular one. I have no energy after dealing with my kids all day. I spend all my time doing stuff for other people. I need some me time, so leave me alone. I deserve it. That's an interesting claim. What exactly do I deserve? These excuses become autonomic responses after a while. Imagine making excuses to justify why I am not growing spiritually. How pathetic am I?

The solution for me is knowing God and growing in intimacy with Him. I always come back to a statement by Frank Laubach in *Practicing His Presence* (a great book that I highly recommend). On Sept. 21, 1930, he wrote in his journal, "It is difficult to convey to another the joy of having broken into the new sea of realizing God's hereness. It seemed so wonderfully true that just the privilege of fellowship with God is infinitely more than anything God could give. When he gives Himself he is giving more than anything else in the universe" (Laubach 1973, 22). If you unfold that concept there is much to learn.

I can only imagine what it would be like spending all that quality time in God's presence, expecting nothing and soaking Him in. Doing this would give us much wisdom and would make us better people. When I hear from God, I know that this is life-changing. He usually speaks in that still small voice, which is oh so elusive. We hear that voice only by having an intimate connection with God. I have learned that the level of intimacy we share with God is up to us to a certain degree. The nearer we draw to God, the nearer He will draw to us. How do I draw near to God? First and foremost, I need to stop sinning. Oh, but it is so much fun to sin. At first it is. That is the struggle Paul talks about in Romans. I do the things I know I shouldn't do, and I don't do the things I know I should do. Why? Because the things I know I shouldn't do are fun.

Here is a truth about that concept. The more intimate you are with God, the less you will want to do those "fun" things, because you will start to view those things the way God does, and they do not look fun after you spend time in His presence. The next step is to believe His Word for yourself and not for someone else. Pray and seek His face. Use all your powers of concentration to come into His presence. A great discipline for me has been journaling. Write down what you are learning from God. Write down answers to prayers, and write out your prayers. Writing adds another level to quiet times.

Fear will creep in as you do all of these things. You need to understand that fear is an enemy of faith, that fear is the real four-letter F-word. You must kick fear to the curb and choose faith.

So how is it possible to stay connected with God on a moment-by-moment basis? Is it difficult? You bet. It is the hardest thing you will ever do. However, when you get there, everything else in your life will become easier because you will be accomplishing tasks through God's power, and it will no longer be you who lives but Christ who lives in and through you. The Bible makes clear how Jesus lived. He was definitely connected with the Father. All day, every day He practiced God's presence, and we are supposed to live as Jesus lived. Here is a promise for you to hold on to. Jesus wants that experience for all of us. He wants us to be in God's presence. In His high priestly prayer from John 17, Jesus tells us all about it. He prays this prayer to the Father on our behalf. Think about that. Jesus is praying for you and for me. If He is praying for us to receive something, we can be assured that it is possible to obtain. That is amazing love! How can it be? I don't know. I only know that Christ's love is meant to be experienced, not understood.

"May you experience the love of Christ, though it is too great to understand fully. Then you will be made complete with all the fullness of life and power that comes from God" (Ephesians 3:19 NLT). I want to experience that love through intimacy with Jesus. I need to practice His presence with perseverance and fervor. I need to get serious about it and understand that it doesn't happen at the speed of today's technology.

God, help me to set my mind on You and on what You want me to pursue. Help me to say yes to Your will and to Your way, for Your ways are much greater than mine. I know my flesh and my mind are weak. Protect me from the things that attack those weaknesses. Help me to remember You throughout my day. Thank You that it is possible to be in Your presence the same way Jesus was when He walked this earth. Thank You, Jesus, that You are praying for me and for all believers that we may be in the Father just as You are in the Father. So be it!

> My prayer is not for them alone. I pray also for those who will believe in me through their message, that all of them may be one, Father, just as you are in me and I am in you. May they also be in us so that the world may believe that you have sent me. I have given them the glory that you gave me, that they may be one as we are one—I in them and you in me—so that they may be brought to complete unity. Then the world

> will know that you sent me and have loved them even
> as you have loved me. (John 17:20–23 NIV)

We are "those who will believe in me" through the message that has been handed down about Jesus. I thank Him for making this intimate relationship possible.

Press on...

DEEP SPIRITUAL THOUGHT #873

Promises, Promises

Do you ever wonder if the promises in God's Word are for you? Do you sometimes think they are for someone else?

What is a promise? It can be used as a noun, as in a promise given, or as a verb, as in "I promise." When we refer to God's promises, we are talking about God's declarations to do or not to do something. When we talk about the Bible, we are referring to God's Word. The declarations God makes in the Bible, or others make as a result of knowing Him intimately, are meant for everyone.

When we experience God supplying our needs with His riches, we grow closer to Him because we see the promise kept. The more we grow in God's presence, the more we can claim these promises, which are written throughout His Word. The promise in Jeremiah 29:11 comes to mind: God has plans to prosper us and not to harm us, plans to give us hope and a future. And the psalmist says in 37:4 that if we delight ourselves in the Lord, He will give us the desires of our hearts. When our hearts are aligned with God's, His desires for us become our desires. The promises in His Word are for us. Another that comes to mind is in Hebrews 4:16, which says we can go boldly to God's throne to find grace.

There are many promises in Scripture, and they are all mine. I can claim them by faith. But there's more.

While reading His Word, I learned something new about the promises that God has given us. I learned about the why. Why has God given us these promises? The answer came in this passage:

"By His divine power, God has given us everything we need for living a godly life. We have received all of this by coming to know Him, the one who called us to Himself by means of His marvelous glory and excellence. And because of His glory and excellence, He has given us great and precious promises. These are the promises that enable you to share His divine nature and escape the world's corruption caused by human desire" (2 Peter 1:3–4 NLT).

He gave us these promises so that we would be able to share in His divine nature and become more like Jesus. We can become more like Jesus by believing and claiming these promises. Jesus certainly believed God's promises and clung to them. He was probably given a promise specific before He took a trip to our planet. He was probably told something like, "No matter what happens, Son, I promise to take care of You. No matter how badly they beat You, or even if they kill You, it is a part of My plan to save them from themselves. I promise You that the world will be saved through You. Even if it feels like I have left You, I will never do that. I promise You." God makes good on even the loftiest promises. His word is His bond, and His promises are nothing but the truth.

These promises cause us to be more like Jesus when we believe, claim them, and live them out. They help us to escape the world's corruption caused by human desires. All of these promises were fulfilled by Jesus' final words on the cross: it is finished. The prophecies are fulfilled, delivery from death is ours, and abundant life is ours through His love.

This next passage explains what happens when we respond to God's promises.

"In view of all this, make every effort to respond to God's promises. Supplement your faith with a generous provision of moral excellence, and moral excellence with knowledge, and knowledge with self-control, and self-control with patient endurance, and patient endurance with godliness, and godliness with brotherly affection, and brotherly affection with love for everyone. The more you grow like this, the more productive and useful you will be in your knowledge of our Lord Jesus Christ" (2 Peter 1:5–8 NLT). And that is the formula!

There is so much packed into those verses that the passage must be broken down and prayed upon. Ask yourself some questions as you pray: God, do I possess a generous provision of moral excellence? Is that me? Do I possess knowledge of you in ever-increasing measure? Do I have self-control? After all, this is a fruit of the Spirit. What about the rest? Do I possess patient endurance? Am I godly? Do I love my brothers and sisters in Christ? Search me, God, and know my heart, and help me to do better in the areas that You have just exposed.

I keep asking myself what I hope to accomplish in all this. I want to understand God's promises so much so that I get to share His divine nature and to escape the world's corruption caused by my own selfish desires. I want God to expose those to me. I want to become more like Jesus every day, to keep advancing from one degree of glory to the next. My goal is to be completely in tune with God's voice, His promises, His Holy Spirit, and His gifts, and to live out my life based on those promises. I want God to be my vision. I want to walk as Jesus walked, in full submission to the will of the Father.

The more I get to know God, the more I want to be like Jesus. I also find the more I get to know God, the fewer complex questions I have. I gain more wisdom in practical day-to-day living. I am not as stressed as I used to be. I trust God more with my future. I used to want to control every area of my life, but the more I get to know God, the less I want to control. God has the best plan for me, and I need to live out that plan one day at a time. The more I trust in God's promises, the more I am learning to share in His divine nature and escaping the world's corruption caused by human desires.

Thanks be to God for His promises. Thank God that every promise in the Bible can be mine by faith.

Press on...

Good Friday or Bad Friday?
It Depends on Perspective

Perhaps you have wondered, *If Friday was the day Jesus died, why do we call it good? Why isn't it called Bad Friday, or Dark Friday, or Black Friday?* We call it Good Friday from our perspective in history. We know the full story of the cross. We know of all the good that came about as a result of the cross. On that Friday Jesus hung on the cross, taking the place of every sinner who would ever live, including me. He suffered and bled for my sake and for yours. He made the ultimate sacrifice for sins once and for all time. That indeed is a good thing viewed from this side of history.

But what if you were looking at it from a different perspective? What if you were alive on that Friday when Jesus was to be nailed to that tree? What would your perspective be if you were one of His followers on that Friday that changed history? Let's go on a mental journey and stretch our minds to see what that Friday might look like to a follower of Jesus somewhere around the year 33.

So here you are, following Jesus around, listening to Him teach, seeing the miracles He performs, and hearing Him drop hints about His death. You thought that would happen when He was old. You didn't understand the urgency in Jesus' teaching. It wasn't until after His death that you started putting all the pieces of the puzzle together. "All I know is what I saw that day," you recall, "and it was far from good. I saw my teacher, my healer, punished for crimes He didn't commit. In fact, I saw Him suffer the worst punishment possible, one usually reserved for the worst criminals. I saw him being beaten within an inch of His life. I saw Him whipped and forced to carry a part of a tree on his back. I saw soldiers do horrible things to my Jesus that day, things I can't even repeat. I saw Him crucified. I saw them slaughter my Jesus. I cannot even begin to share with you the pain I felt that day, the agony, the emotional suffering, as I saw my teacher being treated the way He was.

"After all the beatings, I heard the cries of Jesus. I kept thinking, *What can I do? How can I help? Alas, I cannot.* I then saw the soldiers driving spikes through His hands and saw the cross being raised. I felt nothing but despair. I kept thinking, *This is not fair. He didn't do anything.* Then I heard Jesus cry out in a loud voice, saying it was finished. He committed His spirit to the Father, and He was gone.

"At that point it seemed as if all hell broke loose. The skies darkened, there was an earthquake, rocks were split in two, tombs burst open, and the bodies of many sleeping holy men and women were raised up. Then I saw one of the most significant things I had ever seen. I saw the temple veil being ripped apart. This was such an important event because the temple was the place where God was said to have lived. The temple sanctuary was divided into two sections—the holy place and the most holy place. The most holy place was considered so holy that only the high priest could enter, and only once a year. The curtain that I saw rip down the middle separated these two areas. The curtain that was meant to protect us from the power of God's presence was ripped apart by the death of Jesus. I remember thinking, *Wow! This is incredibly significant. God is now giving us access to Himself as a result of Jesus' sacrificial death.* There was so much going on that I couldn't get it all as it was unfolding. I think I am in a bit of shock, and I need time to reflect on all the events of that day."

That must have been how the disciples of Jesus felt. It probably took a little time to piece all of this together.

It is extremely hard to look at Good Friday through the eyes of someone who doesn't know what happened on Easter Sunday, but it is important to reflect on this perspective and to figure out what it means to you. That is how I will approach Good Fridays from now on. I will use the day, and the days leading up to it, for quiet reflection It is like no other day in history. I will remember Christ's precious blood as it was spilled for me and will be extremely thankful. I will remember His beaten-down and broken body and the suffering He endured for me, and I will be extremely thankful.

As much as possible I want to remember the day not only as if I was one of His followers in the crowd but as if I was one of His chosen disciples, or His brother, or His mother. What a Friday it must have been for them. The smell of death filled the air, and darkness overtook the land for a couple of hours. What do you suppose that smelled like? What would darkness look like in the middle of the day? I think it would be like total separation from God—like hell.

Now that is perspective. Yesterday I was complaining about spiritual dryness (that was my big issue), whereas today (Friday) the disciples are seeing their teacher/savior taken from them in brutal fashion. God, help me on this Friday to understand a little of what that day was really like. Help me to discover what it means to deny myself, to take up my cross, and to follow Jesus. God, I echo Paul's words: "I want to know Christ and experience the mighty power that raised Him from the dead. I want to suffer with Him, sharing in His death" (Philippians 3:10 NLT).

Help me to understand the significance of the prayer I just prayed. Help me to fix my eyes on You, Jesus, as You are the author and perfecter of my faith. Thank You that on this day You chose to take all the sins of the world on Your shoulders—all the sins of the past, present, and future. How incredibly dark that must have been for You, Jesus. I now understand why You cried out, "My God, my God, why have you forsaken me?" You must have felt so dirty and alone with the weight of every sin ever committed on Your shoulders. What incredible love.

God, please create in me a capacity to love more. I want to know more of that great love that caused Jesus to lay down His life for the likes of me, that great love that caused You to send Your only Son to die for me and for everyone else who ever lived and will live. That is an indescribable kind of a love.

This Good Friday take time to reflect on these things. Reflect on what it would have been like if you were there as an observer, then as a disciple. Reflect on what it means to take up your cross daily and to follow Jesus. Reflect on what it means to share in Christ's suffering so you can also share in His resurrection. Reflect on what Jesus must have felt when the sins of the world past, present, and future were piled on Him. Reflect on what love it must have taken for Jesus to willingly die for you when He could have called ten thousand angels to come and defeat His enemies. Reflect on how God has such great love for us that He sent His only Son into this world so that we may live with Him forever. Those who accept this love really will live happily ever after. That is the furthest thing from a fairy tale.

This Good Friday above all else, let us consider Jesus. Let us remember to fix our gaze on Jesus, who gave up all the comforts of heaven to come down to earth and embrace a disgraced death on a cross in our place. Let us remember that He did this and then returned to His Father's right hand. Thank God for Jesus, and thank You, Jesus, for coming and dying in my place. Let us also remember that Sunday is coming, but let's not brush off Friday. Let's reflect on this day even though we know what lies ahead on Sunday.

Press on...

DEEP SPIRITUAL THOUGHT #812

Missing Angels?

He isn't here. He is risen. These were the words of the angel on that first Easter morning. Something scary happened to me as I was reading the account of Easter in the Scriptures: I missed the angels. I was reading and my mind started to wander as it will when I am seeing something familiar. That is sometimes an issue when I read the Bible, so I have to pray before reading that God will keep my mind alert and help me to see what He wants me to see. Anyway, I was reading a passage about the resurrection, and after a little while I realized I had zoned out. When I figure that out, I usually go back to the last place I remember and pick up from there. Using this method, I have sometimes read paragraphs five or six times, but at least I don't miss stuff now. I used this method with the passage about the resurrection, and I realized I had missed the part about the angels. I read right past them. I was reading from John 20, which recounts how Mary Magdalene had a conversation with the angels in the tomb. "She saw two white-robed angels, one sitting at the head and the other at the foot of the place where the body of Jesus had been lying" (John 20:12 NLT).

The first time I read that, I missed the conversation. A sobering thought hit me: it was alarmingly easy for me to skip that passage and miss the angels. I wondered, *Has that ever happened to me in my daily out-and-about life? Have I ever zoned out, even for a brief time, to the point of missing some angels?* I was saddened to think I might I have. Maybe I wasn't alert enough, or watching, or prepared for angels. If God did send angels to me and I failed to see them, remaining "unaware," as the Word says, what spiritual blessings did I miss? Did I alter my spiritual time line? Did I create an alternate spiritual reality, if even for one day?

Why is it so hard to focus on God in the daily routine of life? What else have I missed out on because of my relaxed attitude toward my faith?

This reminded me of Jesus' conversation with His disciples in the garden. He returned to them after going off by Himself to pray and found them asleep on the job. He said to Peter, "Couldn't you watch with me even one hour? Keep watch and pray so that you will not give in to temptation. For the spirit is willing, but the body is weak" (Matthew 26:40–41 NLT).

Jesus, forgive me for falling asleep while waiting for You. Forgive me for not paying enough attention to see Your angels. Help me to watch and to pray. Teach me to be more vigilant in my faith. God, help me to see what You want me to see. Help me to see the world the way You want me to see it. Help me never again to miss Your angels.

My favorite Easter Sunday song is "Up from the Grave He Arose" by Robert Lowry (1826-99). It is such a powerful hymn. "Up from the grave He arose, with a mighty triumph over His foes. He arose a victor from the dark domain, and He lives forever with His saints to reign. He arose, He arose, Hallelujah Christ arose."

Good news: Christ lives with us forever. We are His saints. Death could not keep Him down. Resurrection power is too great. What is even more amazing is God's grace. He made that resurrection power available to all of us.

Paul's prayer for all believers has a lot to say about this. "I also pray that you will understand the incredible greatness of God's power for us who believe Him. This is the same mighty power that raised Christ from the dead and seated him in the place of honor at God's right hand in the heavenly realms" (Ephesians 1:19–20 NLT).

That is a whole lot of power at work within us. Paul later says, "Now all glory to God, who is able, through His mighty power at work within us, to accomplish infinitely more than we might ask or think" (Ephesians 3:20 NLT). What kind of power might we be dealing with? Our minds can't stretch far enough to conceive of the possibilities. Whatever we think up, it's way more than that. Christ said we would do even greater works than He did. Why? Because of that resurrection power that has been made available to us through the Holy Spirit living in us. We have Christ living through us with Holy Spirit power. I don't want to miss another angel, and I want my mind opened to the possibilities.

In the words of Steven Tyler, "I don't want to miss a thing."

The good news is that no matter how bad you are feeling about missing opportunities or angels, there is always the now. God can take all your experiences—good or bad, happy or sad— and use them for His purpose in the now. God can restore anyone and everyone. No matter how bad you think your situation is, God has a plan for restoration. He can restore you and me to the masterpieces that He created us to be, all because of the shed blood of Jesus, all because of His death-defeating act of raising Jesus from the dead. That wonder-working power is available right now.

As a result of spilled blood on a cross on a Friday and an empty tomb on a Sunday, we can live this earthly life to the fullest. We can have abundant life while here on earth. The love of God leads to a fullness of life even while we are here in our earthly bodies with all these earthly rules.

Victory is ours! Our team wins! Every time! We are now more than conquerors because of Jesus! Pay attention. Don't miss the angels!

Press on...

DEEP SPIRITUAL THOUGHT #319

Is Fear Sin?

That is an interesting question that I started asking myself on day seventy-nine of my 365-day experiment in finding intimacy with God. I was thinking that the further I went with this experiment the more I was changing. I realized that my fears were slowly diminishing. I also saw that for every fear I have there is grace enough to cover it. I have learned that if God said it in His Word, it's true. When my thoughts are on God, His grace and peace are near, but when my thoughts turn to fears, sin is lurking. When my thoughts wander in that direction, so does God's nearness. The success of this experiment lies in drawing close to God. Brother Lawrence, a seventeenth-century monk who talked a lot about practicing God's presence, had this to say about the matter: "All things hinge upon your hearty renunciation of everything which you are aware does not lead to God."

That's the secret. I must renounce everything that I know does not bring me closer to God. I must throw off everything that keeps me from His presence, and I need to run the race of life with perseverance, fixing my eyes on Jesus all the way. (See Hebrews 12.)

If my eyes are on Jesus, they won't be on things that lead me to sin. I need to stop sinning. Fear is a sin, and if it is not a sin, it certainly has the potential to lead to sin. I have said throughout my Christian walk that fear is the real four-letter F-word. Fear is the opposite of faith, or the absence of faith. I never equated it to sin until I started drawing nearer to God. I always thought it was one of those emotions that had to be brought into check. I now think it is much more and can lead me out of God's presence. Fear says, "God, this problem of money, health, or relationship is bigger than the promises in your Word to help me with all things and to supply my needs." When I allow my fears to run rampant, I am slapping Jesus across the face. In effect, I am saying, "I don't really trust you, God. My problem is huge." But God is much bigger!

When FEAR (False Evidence Appearing Real) creeps in, I must have faith that the promise is much greater than the problem.

When fear arises, we need to recognize it before it becomes a problem, because fear left unchecked can and will lead to sin. I know this from experience.

I had another firsthand experience with fear as I was praying. I prayed, "Love me, Jesus." I wasn't sure why I used these words. I didn't say this prayer because I was insecure and felt I needed someone to love me. I prayed for Jesus to love me so I could in turn love the people in my life the way Jesus wants me to love them. I never prayed that way before, but I felt compelled, and then it hit me as if a twenty-thousand-watt lightbulb went on over my head. I heard that still small voice saying, "Perfect love casts out all fear." I thought, *There it is, the missing link, the last piece to the jigsaw puzzle.* Just then I heard the "Hallelujah Chorus" playing in the background. I knew I was on to something. I understood why I was praying "Love me, Jesus." It wasn't my love that could cast out fear, because my love is not perfect. But the love of Christ is perfect. I linked that thought with Ephesians 3:19 and realized that Christ's love is the key to fullness of life and the power to live, because it is perfect. This is the love that casts out all fear, and a life without fear is a life lived in the power of the Holy Spirit and the love of Christ. That perfect love is meant to be experienced.

"May you experience the love of Christ though it is too great to fully understand. Then you will be made complete with all the fullness of life and power that comes from God" (Ephesians 3:19 NLT).

The prayer "Love me, Jesus" now makes perfect sense. His love casts out all fear, and that is the love that He wants us to experience. Love me, Jesus!

Press on...

DEEP SPIRITUAL THOUGHT #832

Spiritual Lethargy

Is there such a thing as being spiritually lethargic? I can tell you that spiritual lethargy is real, because I have lived it for several years. Spiritual lethargy is like being a couch potato in your faith. The couch encourages laziness because it is comfortable, familiar, and safe. It won't ask you to get off of it, because it was built for your comfort. Its sole purpose is to give you a comfy place to sit and veg out while watching TV. Yes, you can have good conversations on your couch, and they can be intellectually stimulating, but the main purpose of the couch is to create potatoes.

Spiritual lethargy seems safe, just like being on the couch. But is it really without risk? This condition assumes that you don't have to push yourself or trust God with too much. You can passively go about your Bible reading (when you have time), attend church when it is convenient, and say things like, "I don't have to go to church to be a Christian." That is true and this mind-set works well if your goal is spiritual lethargy. However, meeting with other followers for corporate worship, being inspired in your faith, and setting aside a specific time every week to seek God with others can't be all bad, can it? I know these things to be true because I have experienced them. I have lived in a state of spiritual lethargy for at least seven of the last ten years, so I have become something of an expert in this phenomenon. I am not proud of that, but that is how it was.

Now that I have light in this area and the darkness of lethargy has been lifted, I can see it for what it is.

John 9 tells of Jesus healing a blind man. The Pharisees were eavesdropping on Jesus' conversation and asked Him whether He was saying they were blind. "'If you were blind, you wouldn't be guilty,' Jesus replied, 'but you remain guilty because you claim you can see'" (John 9:41 NLT). Ouch!

When you are stuck in a state of spiritual lethargy as I was, you claim you can still see. But can you? If you aren't involved in a spiritual discipline like reading God's Word on a regular basis, praying, meeting with other believers, or journaling, just to name a few, what can you see?

Can you see anything that resembles God's plan for your life? Not really. You can't see because you have put yourself in a state of partial blindness by pulling away from God. This doesn't happen all at once but slowly over time without you noticing.

The plan is and always has been that if you draw near to God, He will draw near to you. That is the truth of the Word. The opposite must also be true. If you draw away from God through spiritual lethargy, He will draw away from you. At least that is how it will feel. The truth is, you are doing all the drawing away while Jesus is calling you to come closer.

You are still saved during this process of drawing away, but the more you draw away from God, the more you open yourself up to sin. Stagnation sets in, and that is dangerous. Think about what happens to stagnating water. That is no way to live the Christian life. The Christian life is all about being an overcomer and receiving victory. It is about being more than a conqueror, not about stagnating your way to a slow death or complete loss of faith.

Spiritual lethargy is not a good plan. In fact, it is no plan. Doing nothing in your faith will lead you down this path. Spiritual lethargy brings temporary spiritual blindness, which can lead to stagnation and eventually to spiritual death. This happens when your faith is simply about getting by in this life. You believe just enough to get into heaven. You say, "I don't have to practice my faith to be a Christian, and I don't have to go to church to prove that I am a Christian." That is the path of spiritual lethargy. You live a life of spiritual deprivation and starvation, and nothing good comes from this. The sad part is that it may take a major crisis to see this in yourself. At least that is how it was with me. God had to shake me pretty hard to get me out of my spiritual lethargy, but I am thankful that He did.

Heed the warning signs when you see them. Perhaps you don't read the Word as much as you should because you find it boring and tedious. Maybe you aren't praying as you once did. Perhaps you are not taking advantage of some other spiritual discipline the way you once did. Take time to do a self-evaluation. Then ask God to search you. I prayed every day for about a month and still do from time to time for God to search me, to know my heart, to point out any area in my life that doesn't please Him, and to help me to change it. This was the beginning of my reawakening. The great news is that it doesn't matter where you are now. God can do a new thing. He can wake up old visions or dreams He may have planted in your heart. Turn your eyes toward Jesus even a little bit, and you will find He is intently looking back at you, with open arms. The time is now to evaluate yourself and if necessary to snap out of a spiritual lethargy and turn toward Jesus. He began a good work in you, and He will be faithful to complete it. That is a promise you can take to the bank.

Around 1685 a monk named Brother Lawrence made a statement that has reverberated throughout history. He talked a lot about how to maintain a relationship with Christ on a day-to-day basis. In all my reading about this monk, I could find no evidence of spiritual lethargy. He was in such close contact with Christ every day that he would never put himself in such danger. This quote from him gives us an idea of how we too can live a satisfying Christian experience and never let our faith grow cold or allow ourselves to become spiritually lethargic. He said, "I cannot imagine how a Christian can live a satisfied Christian experience without the practice of being in the presence of Christ."

That is the key to ending the epidemic of spiritual lethargy in the Christian church today. Guard your hearts against this and remember that "He who began a good work in you will carry it on to completion until the day of Christ Jesus" (Philippians 1:6 NIV).

Press on...

If you are wondering why I use "Press on" as a closing, read this passage.

> I want to know Christ—yes, to know the power of his resurrection and participation in his sufferings, becoming like him in his death, and so, somehow, attaining to the resurrection from the dead. Not that I have already obtained all this, or have already arrived at my goal, but I press on to take hold of that for which Christ Jesus took hold of me. Brothers and sisters, I do not consider myself yet to have taken hold of it. But one thing I do: Forgetting what is behind and straining toward what is ahead, I press on toward the goal to win the prize for which God has called me heavenward in Christ Jesus. (Philippians 3:10–14 NIV)

"Press on" reminds me to stay away from spiritual lethargy, to forget what is behind me, and to focus on what is ahead. I press on to win the prize for which God has called me heavenward in Christ Jesus. So for now ...

Press on...

DEEP SPIRITUAL THOUGHT #733

That Lingering Presence

Were you ever a smoker? Do you remember the terrible smell the smoke left on your clothes? Even as a smoker I thought, *This stuff smells really bad*. That was the aftereffect. While I was smoking I didn't notice a bad smell. I would be engrossed in my cigarette and my thoughts. I would sit alone and try to blow the perfect smoke ring. I also remember the coughing and the stained teeth and the foul taste in my mouth all the time, not to mention all the money I was spending. It was the equivalent of holding a ten-dollar bill in my hand and lighting it on fire. The next day I would light another ten and so on. I was doing worse than that because there are no health risks in burning a ten-dollar bill unless you drench it in gas first or you are married.

I finally got enough sense to quit. When I did, I was one of the worst ex-smokers ever. Anyone who dared to smoke around me got an earful. What stood out most for me was the smell. Whenever I was around it, the smell seemed to be about fifty times worse than when I was smoking myself. I started observing the smoke. I watched it chase people down the road. Smoke has the tendency to do that, at least when there is a slight wind blowing in the same direction. When you are walking into a mall and the wind is blowing lightly in your face, you smell the smoke long before you see the smoker. The smell is especially noticeable while you are leaving a smoking area. I was walking away from a store one day while someone was smoking outside. The smell stayed with me, and just when I thought it had dissipated, I got another whiff, and it was terrible. I hate the smell of smoke.

I have been on a quest to be in God's presence, to practice His presence, and to stay there. Doing this has parallels with the lingering smell of smoke.

Do you know someone who practices God's presence and seems to radiate His Spirit? I have met a few people like this. One was an elderly lady who was a prayer warrior. She spent most of her days and nights praying. How do I know that? I could see it all over her face. She radiated God's presence when I talked to her, and her speech was always God-honoring. Every time I was in contact with her I felt the Lord's presence. Another person like this was a retired pastor and professor whom I had the privilege of hearing speak. I could tell this man not only knew God but also knew about being in His presence. I had a chance to interview him. I didn't necessarily want to learn more about some of the things he said. Instead I wanted to learn how he prepared, since I was a young pastor at the time. He was obviously a learned man, but I didn't want to know how he did his research or where he got his sources. I wanted to know how he knew God so well. I could tell that he was speaking out of the overflow of his heart.

"A good person produces good things from the treasury of a good heart, and an evil person produces evil things from the treasury of an evil heart. What you say flows from what is in your heart" (Luke 6:45 NLT).

The overflow of his heart came solely from God. How do you get to that point? The answers I received to my questions were simple but practical. I will never forget what he told me. He said, "Before I preach I go away to be alone with God for several hours." At this event, the setting was a nature walk. He had found a clearing with a neat tree in the middle and had sat down and prayed. I could tell by his sermon that he had just been in God's presence. I noticed it in his face as he preached. He had a passion that was transferred through a glow. His demeanor was relaxed, and he was comfortable speaking about God and about being in His presence. Many years later I still remember my response to that sermon. I wanted to get closer to God, to know Him better, and to be consistent in spending time alone with Him every day.

I failed miserably. Life got in the way, and I acquiesced. The good news is that our God is full of grace and mercy and that He never leaves us. He stays with us through the tough times, through all the times when we find ourselves pulling away from Him. He loves us so much that He continues to work with us and to restore us if necessary.

So what does this have to do with the lingering effects of smoke? Just as the smoke stays on us, so do the effects of being in God's presence. You can see the aftereffects on someone who has met with God. They seem to stick to us and follow us around. That is what I noticed in this man many years ago. I saw the effects of being in God's presence. I could see them on his face, in his body language, in his words, in the way he moved. I could see God's presence lingering in him just like cigarette smoke would. Cigarette smoke takes awhile to go away, and God's presence has the same quality. It usually takes a little while for the effects to wear off, depending on what we are doing in our day.

Wouldn't it be something if we could live our lives like this all the time? We could start the day in God's presence and go to work with the lingering effects of our time with Him. When that wore off we could try to work in more quiet time throughout the day. This is tough because we are selfish. Even when we pray we are sometimes selfish. We sometimes want what God can give us or do for us more than we want His presence. We must come to the point where we can say: it is no longer I who lives but Christ who lives in me. That is my prayer. I want to be so much in God's presence that people will see the lingering effects. I want to be so caught up in His presence that it is no longer I who lives but Christ who lives in me.

This can be done only in solitude and quiet time with God. You must make an effort to break free from the things of the world long enough to be in His presence. You need to examine yourself and pray that God will search your heart to see if anything there displeases Him. Remember that what you put in your heart will eventually come out of your mouth. Guard what goes into your heart. Be in God's presence!

Press on...

DEEP SPIRITUAL THOUGHT #291

A Day Like Today

Just when I thought I was getting better at focusing my thoughts and concentrating on God, along comes a day like today.

It started with doubts, and then as I was reading Scripture (John 13–15 from where I got this thought), I discovered the disciples of Jesus also were full of doubts. In John 13 and 14, Jesus has a conversation with them. At the end of chapter 13, Jesus tells Peter that he will deny three times that he knows Jesus. Ouch! In chapter 14 Jesus says He is going away to heaven to prepare rooms. He tells the disciples that they know the way. Speaking for the others, Thomas replies that they don't even know where He is going. (At this point I was thinking, *Wow! You guys still don't know. He has been talking to you about this stuff for a while.*)

So Jesus again has to spell it out for them and for us. Jesus tells them that He is the way and follows it up by saying that He is also the truth and the life and that the only way anyone can get to the Father is through Him.

That should have been enough, but Phillip then asks Jesus to show them the Father. Jesus is getting a little perturbed and says in effect, "What? I have been with you guys for all this time and you still don't know who I am?" In the next few verses Jesus talks about God speaking through Him and how the works He has done were from the Father. He goes on to say that we will do greater works and that we can ask anything in His name and God will do it so the Son can bring glory to the Father.

There is long way to go from "you guys still don't know me" to "greater works" to "ask anything in my name." Closing the gaps requires a huge grace bridge. It must be pure grace for God to deal with us and our unbeliefs, fears, and doubts. Some days I feel very close to Jesus, while on others I feel further away and have doubts and fears. On those days Jesus seems to speak to me the same way He did to the disciples.

Sometimes it even feels as if Jesus is saying to me, "Have I been with you all this time, Trevor, and you still don't know who I am?" That is how I felt today. Jesus, I want to get to know You better every day by obeying You and trusting You. I can pull this off only when You live Your life through me.

Thank You that You offer us a solution. You offer us Your Holy Spirit to live in and through us. Then we can experience peace, the kind that surpasses our understanding and answers all of our fears, doubts, and unbeliefs.

The following passage gives us the solution to our doubts about Jesus and to our fears and unbeliefs.

> If you love me, obey my commandments and I will ask the Father, and He will give you another Advocate, who will never leave you. He is the Holy Spirit, who leads into all truth ... you know him because he lives with you now [Jesus], and later will be in you ... When I am raised to life again, you will know that I am in the Father, and you are in me, and I am in you ... And remember, my words are not my own. What I am telling you is from the Father who sent me ... But when the Father sends the Advocate as my representative—that is, the Holy Spirit—he will teach you everything I have told you. I am leaving

you with a gift—peace of mind and heart. And the
peace I give is a gift the world cannot give. So don't
be troubled or afraid ... but I will do what the Father
requires of me, so that the world will know that I love
the Father. Come, let's be going. (John 14:15–17, 20,
24, 26–27, 31 NLT)

So the next time you start doubting, remember that the
disciples doubted even when Jesus lived among them. However,
after they received Christ's promises in their conversation with
Him, they were totally changed. They lived their lives in the
power of Jesus' Spirit and were bold in their witness.

I guess there is still hope for me Come, Holy Spirit!

Press on...

DEEP SPIRITUAL THOUGHT #635

All We Need Is Love

It was confirmed again this morning as I was reading John 15: everything begins and ends with God's love. Apart from His love we cannot do anything. We will not produce any fruit without this love.

How do we get this love? It comes to us from being in the presence of Jesus and by remaining there.

Okay, let's back up a minute. Jesus says that He is the vine, that God is the gardener, and that our role is to be the branches. Then He says, "But if you remain in me and my words remain in you, you may ask anything you want, and it will be granted" (John 15:7 NLT).

So the "anything you ask" clause must come as a result of remaining in His presence and Jesus remaining in us.

That sounds easy enough, but how can we remain in His love? That seems to indicate an ongoing deal. How can we remain in anything? We seem to be suffering from a form of attention deficit disorder when it comes to staying put. The answer is quite simple. Our job is to be obedient to what God says. If we obey His commands, we will remain in His love. That is the formula for joy.

Okay, now we are getting somewhere. We know how we can remain in His love and be filled with joy. We need to obey the commandments of Jesus, because when we do that, we remain in His love just as Jesus remained in God's love when He obeyed His Father's commandments. As a result of this new knowledge, we have the potential to overflow with joy, an added benefit.

Let's take this a step further and figure out what we do with this love once we remain in it. John 15:12 gives us definite clues, telling us we need to love each other. This love means being willing to die for each other. That is radical love; that is Jesus love. We can live out this love only in the power of the Holy Spirit.

Our questions are being answered now, even before we ask them. Jesus is fitting all His statements together for our understanding. The tricky part is that we cannot produce this type of love on our own. Only by allowing Jesus to live His life through us can we show the kind of love He describes. This isn't merely hard to do. It is impossible for us to do out of our own ambition or in our own strength. So we have a couple of options.

The first option says: I am going to give up. I can't produce this kind of love. I don't get it. I haven't been able to remain in Jesus' presence long enough to get to that next level. It just isn't in me.

Of course it isn't. This love isn't in us unless Jesus is in us.

The second option says: I want to experience this love, which cannot be understood with our finite nature. I want what Paul prayed for in Ephesians.

> And may you have the power to understand, as all God's people should, how wide, how long, how high, and how deep his love is. May you experience the love of Christ, though it is too great to understand fully. Then you will be made complete with all the fullness of life and power that comes from God. Now all glory to God, who is able, through his mighty power at work within us, to accomplish infinitely more than

we might ask or think. Glory to him in the church and in Christ Jesus through all generations forever and ever. Amen! (Ephesians 3:18–21 NLT)

All we need is love, the right kind of love. We need to experience Jesus' love. Then we can obey His commandment to love each other as He loved us. When Jesus summed up the law, He said it was all about love. Love God with all your heart, soul, strength, and mind. Then love others the same way you love yourself.

Press on...

Connecting the Dots

The diagram is love. The dots are the connecting points or the results of the love flow. The love I am talking about is Christ's love. That's the love I want to experience, though it is too great to fully understand. The kind of love that forgives my sins. The kind of love that causes someone to lay down his life for his friends. A supernatural love. A love that cannot be intellectualized. A love that accepts faults. A love that embraces the unlovable. A love that extends to enemies. A love that is pure with no form of manipulation tied to it. True love.

That is the kind of love I want to know and to experience all the time. A love that I can feel as a result of a heart that overflows with Christ's love and spills into the world around me. A love for my fellow believers that proves to the world that we are followers of Christ. They will know we are Christians by our love. But do they? Do we care? Are we really concerned if our friends, coworkers, and acquaintances know we are Christians? How is all this possible?

We can love only because God first loved us. We need to accept that love and remain in it. When we remain in that love, we are filled with joy that overflows. While living in that love, we become Christ's modern-day disciples, His hands and feet in this world. "The world will hate you," says Jesus, "just as it hated Me," but He tells us to take heart, because ultimately He overcomes the world. (Throughout his book, by the way, John interprets "the world" as those who actively oppose God.)

Okay, let me try to absorb this great concept. Jesus loves me, and He wants to be in me and I in Him just as the Father is in Him and He is in the Father. That is pretty cool. He wants the love that He gives me to overflow from my heart and to spill out of my mouth, changing my words. I want to speak the words of love and grace that Jesus spoke. I also need to understand that there is a whole team of people who want the same thing. They are called Christians. I need to love Christians more than I do. I know that seems like an absurd statement, but there is a lot of truth in it. I sometimes have a harder time loving my fellow Christians than I do those people outside of the faith. Why is that? I believe it is because my standards for judging are higher for those inside the faith. Right or wrong, that is what happens. I tend to judge those inside the faith when I should be saying, "We are all on the same team. We all have similar goals. We may have different methods, but our hearts are going in the same direction. God, help me to love more deeply and to care about the things that You care about more of the time."

The question remains: how do I do these things? It is easy to talk about it, but how do I love more? I think the answer first involves the mind. I must set my mind on things above. I have to focus my thoughts on the love, grace, and mercy that have been poured out for me. I have to offer that same grace and mercy to those inside the faith as well as outside. How will the world (those who actively oppose God) know we are Christians if they do not see this love?

Reading about Brother Lawrence, the seventeenth-century monk, I discovered an interesting feature of his character. When Brother Lawrence finished his work, he examined his performance. If he had done well, he gave thanks to God. If he found otherwise, he asked forgiveness, and without being discouraged he set his mind right again. Brother Lawrence commented, "Thus by rising after my falls, and by frequently renewing my acts of faith and love, I have come to a state wherein it would be difficult for me not to think of God as it was at first to accustom myself to think of Him" (Laubach 1973, 103).

If Brother Lawrence took that much care at work, where we are usually on autopilot, how much more would he be focused on God when involved in the other areas of his life? He said that he had trained himself to think of God throughout his workday. What a statement! We like to compartmentalize these days. Work is here, family is here, and playtime is over there. We have learned to separate who we are into roles and categories. Brother Lawrence thought about God in every area of his life and approached every situation by thinking about God first.

That is the key. I have been on this journey of practicing God's presence for quite a while, and it was harder at first than it is today. I started out by telling myself, *This is really difficult. It must have been easier for Brother Lawrence because he was living in the 1600s and never had anything else to do.* Then I am honest with myself and realize I am making excuses. I have twenty-four hours in the day, just as he did. He had a job; I have a job. He chose to think about God throughout his day. I am working on it.

The good news is that the journey of practicing God's presence gets easier with time. The more time you spend focusing on God and not on stuff, the easier the stuff of life gets. Weird but true.

So how do I love more? It all comes down to time spent at the feet of Jesus. Take time out today and think about God as He relates to your job. When you are done working, think about God as you are about to go to the gym or to spend time with your family. Is what you do next out of love and God-honoring? Think about it.

Press on...

DEEP SPIRITUAL THOUGHT #037

"It Is *Finished*" *Healing*

Softly and slowly say the word *healing*. The word sounds relaxing and soothing, especially if you whisper it with your eyes closed. Now say it aloud and add the word *power* to the end. The phrase isn't as relaxing and soothing, because it conjures up more intense thoughts. A gentle process becomes something that commands attention. If you were to say "healing power through the blood of Christ" in a loud voice, you might have yet another reaction depending on your level of faith. You might laugh mockingly, or you might doubt what you had just said. You might say, "I believe there is healing power in the blood but not for me." You might say, "Healing power through the blood? That would be nice. I would sure like healing in some areas of my life." Others would say, "Healing? What exactly do you mean by that? There are many types of healing. There is physical healing, emotional healing, spiritual healing, and so on. Which do you mean?"

This is true. There are different types of healing. My thinking on healing has changed over the years, and this morning as I was reading I discovered that what I think about healing isn't necessarily what I profess to believe about it. I realized that I don't quite have the faith required for this. I now understand that fear and unbelief have always kept me back. Healing is one of those areas where I believe but need help with my unbelief.

We tend to ask ourselves, *What if God doesn't want me healed?* So accepting healing becomes tricky. A lot of the time the problem is our unbelief.

God has been connecting the dots for me while I have been practicing His presence. I have been thinking lately about the verse that says we must walk as Jesus walked. Sure enough it showed up in my devotions this morning. "For God called you to do good, even if it means suffering, just as Christ suffered for you. He is your example and you must follow in His steps" (1 Peter 2:21 NLT). (This is the verse that inspired the book *In His Steps*.) We must walk as Christ walked. But how did He walk?

Jesus never sinned nor deceived anyone. He did not retaliate when He was insulted or threaten revenge when He suffered. He left His case in the hands of God, who always judges fairly. He carried our sins in His body on the cross so that we can be dead to sin and live for what is right. By His wounds we are healed. Once we were like sheep who wandered away, but now we have turned to our Shepherd, the guardian of our souls. Walking as He walked is a tall order, and we can never do this perfectly. That is not the point. Our goal must be to take on His character. By Jesus' actions on the cross we can do just that. With that "It is finished" moment, every promise in Scripture can become our reality. We can take on the character of Christ and walk as He walked in a sense.

God's promises include every kind of healing that we could possibly need. We are now healed even from death. This is the ultimate healing. Because of Christ's wounds, death isn't the end for us. The same resurrection power that was available to Christ is now available to us. This death healing, or "It is finished" healing as I call it, encompasses all healing. I never quite understood the depths of that until now. With death healing we never die but live eternally. Sometimes healing comes to us in a change of perspective, but faith in this "It is finished" healing makes it possible for us to be healed while living on earth.

That includes every form of healing. What do you want to be healed from today? "It is finished" healing has you covered. You just need the faith to believe it. Keep in mind that healing may not look the way you have envisioned it, but if you believe and allow it, you will be healed. You may still live with the infirmity as was the case with Paul. However, his perspective changed from "This is what I want" to "Your will be done." That is healing in the greatest sense. When we can submit our agendas to God's plan, we have been healed to the fullest extent. Once our perspective changes, everything else changes. Our ultimate healing comes from the blood of Jesus Christ and from His wounds. That blood covers over all our sin and gives us access to "It is finished" healing.

This gift of healing works in conjunction with God's will. Some people are healed so others can believe that Jesus is the Christ, the Son of the living God and so glory can be given. Are others not healed so people won't believe? Of course not. We just don't understand the way God does. Our minds can't quite get there. That is why we need faith to say to the unbeliever, "I was healed—not physically, but since I have been praying for healing, this is what has happened in my mind and in my emotions."

"It is finished" healing completes Jesus' earthly ministry (in bodily form) and enables the Bible to come to life. All the prophecies about Jesus were fulfilled with His death and resurrection, and every promise is now made available for those who believe that Jesus is the Christ, the Son of the living God, and who have invited Him to live in their hearts. How do we know what promise to claim? When we pray and seek God's will, He shows us what He wants for us, but we must start by drawing near to Him so that He will draw near to us.

That is where my journey began 116 days ago. I prayed, "God, help me to draw near to You so that You will draw near to me." Closeness to God fills in all the blanks that need to be filled in.

He will do it. God will give you the ideas and the opportunities. And these things will probably differ from the picture you have in your mind. That I can tell you from experience. What God shows me is usually different from what I imagine—and better. That's all because of "It is finished" healing.

We must walk as Jesus walked. We can do that if we allow Christ to live in us and to take control and if we believe in "It is finished" power. My goal is to get so connected to Jesus, to walk so close to Him, that I no longer recognize the selfish me. I want to be able to say that it is no longer I who lives but Christ who lives in me. I want that to be evident for others to see. That is possible because it is finished. Because it is finished, it is started for me and for all who accept that new life. Thank You, Jesus, for Your "It is finished" healing.

Press on...

DEEP SPIRITUAL THOUGHT #226

Does God Hear My Prayers?

"I prayed to the Lord and He answered me. He freed me from all my fears" (Psalm 34:4 NLT).

"In my desperation I prayed, and the Lord listened, he saved me from all my troubles" (Psalm 34:6 NLT).

Why? Because "the eyes of The Lord watch over those who do right, his ears are open to their cries for help" (Psalm 34:15 NLT).

Well, that confirms it. God does hear my prayers after all. First He frees me from all my fears. These usually consist of the stuff that hasn't happened to me yet, though I think it might. In freeing me from these worries, God has done me a great service. Fear has the potential to freeze me in my tracks. It is an evil thing. Verse 4 talks about praying to the Lord and being answered. Then the psalmist says, "He freed me from all my fears." That opens up a line of communication between me and God. Knowing that He has freed me from my fears helps me to relax and increases my faith. I gain great confidence, knowing I don't have to fear anymore.

Then God saves me from all my trouble, the stuff that is happening to me (v. 6).

The answers to my prayers vary, but based on these verses, I know that God hears all of my prayers. The answers include but are not limited to: a) yes; b) no; that plan isn't good for you, but I have a better one; c) not yet; wait and trust me. Sometimes you may wait decades for certain prayers to come to fruition. Perhaps prayers prayed by your great-great-grandparents are now producing results. God is not confined by our time and our schedules. Prayers could be in play for hundreds of years before they are realized in our realm. This is an incredible thought. Time does not come into play when we pray. That is why it is imperative that we learn how to rest. Resting doesn't mean forgetting or doing nothing. It means continuing to pray, focusing on the thing you are praying for, and trusting that God will provide a solution at some point (either in this life or in the one to come). We often pray as if something were a limited-time offer. We need to understand that our prayers exit our linear time and head into a completely different realm.

The book of Daniel contains a good example. An angel comes to Daniel and explains that God has heard his prayers. However, the angel was detained in the other realm and apologizes for the delay.

"Then he continued, Do not be afraid Daniel. Since the first day that you set your mind to gain understanding and to humble yourself before your God, your words were heard, and I have come in response to them. But the prince of the Persian kingdom resisted me twenty-one days. Then Michael, one of the chief princes, came to help me, because I was detained there with the king of Persia" (Daniel 10:12–13 NIV).

I don't know what happens in the spiritual realm when we pray, but it seems to cause a real stir. The spiritual realm gets engaged and stuff happens. But it happens in God's time.

I am glad that God has perfect timing. Thank You, God, for the promises in Your Word, including the promise that You hear our prayers. Thank You for listening and for answering. I thank You for all the times You didn't give me exactly what I wanted and treat me like a spoiled child. I want what You want. I want to know what You want me to know. Your Word tells me to pray about everything. Thank You that You listen to everything. That is so amazing.

Do you ever catch yourself blocking out people when they are talking? Maybe they are annoying because they ramble on and never shut up. I know I do that, and I am sure at times we all do. God doesn't do that. He listens to every word. Amazing. I am having a hard time wrapping my mind around that, but it is the truth. Thank You, God, for listening when I ramble and when I pray about everything. Thank You that You never fail me if I put all my trust in You. You are my hope for myself and for my family. You are my hope for all healing whether it be physical, emotional, mental, or otherwise. You are my retirement plan. You are my transportation. In You I live and move and have my being. You are my inspiration and my motivation. You are my protection against illness. You lift my head when I do fall ill. You are my all in all. You are my strength for today and my hope for tomorrow. You are my provider. You are my housing. You are my finances. You are my counselor.

Thank You that You speak to me every day through Your Word, through Your world, through other people, and through the still small voice of the Holy Spirit. Help me to hear You more clearly with each passing day.

Thank You that You are my all in all. Thank You for "It is finished" perspective!

Press on...

DEEP SPIRITUAL THOUGHT #475

Tears in a Bottle?

As I was praying this morning in the book of Psalms, this verse leaped out at me. "You keep track of all my sorrows. You have collected all my tears in your bottle. You have recorded each one in your book" (Psalm 56:8 NLT). Say what?

This powerful verse spoke volumes to me. It was written by David in one of his times of duress. This verse speaks about just how much God loves us. It shows us that God keeps track of us. He knows what we are up to. He knows when we cry even one tear. We see a great image of God's compassion here. He has collected all our tears in a bottle and made a record of each one. How much does God care about us? Do we even remotely get it? How much does He love us? How humbling it is to begin to grasp this concept.

This image is even more significant than the idea that the hairs on our heads are numbered. That idea deals with how well God knows us, whereas the tears recorded in the book signify how much He cares for us. What a personal God we serve. I definitely want to know more about the God who keeps track of my tears, stores them in a bottle, and writes them in His book. What an honor to be able to have a personal relationship with such a loving and caring God. Words can't begin to express how great and significant this is. That is the problem sometimes when dealing with such an incredible God. His love is too hard to put into words.

David's writings underscore his close relationship with God. God knows where David has been, where he is going, and what kind of trouble he is in. David knows God will turn those tears of sorrow into tears of joy at just the right time. That is how God relates to us as well.

He sees our sorrows, He counts our tears, He writes them in His journal, and at just the right moment, in his time, He will turn those tears of sorrow into tears of joy. The timing is up to God, and our responsibility is to get to know more of this God who cares so much for us that He counts our tears.

David knew that God would rescue him from his troubles. Why? Because every time that David had gotten into trouble, God showed up, and David knew that a God who counted and recorded his tears could definitely rescue him from his enemies. God will do the same for us.

It is up to us to come to God with our tears of sorrow and say, "God, I give You my tears of sorrow, and I trust that in Your time, You will replace them with tears of joy. I do not know the how, but I know the who and the why."

I want to know more of that tear-saving, tear-recording God and experience Him in my boring day-to-day life as well as in my exciting days. Thank You that You are that kind of a God, and help me to understand what that means for me today.

Press on...

If I Had Only One Book

If I could read only one more book for the rest of my life, what would it be? John Wesley said he was a man of one book. This was debated in a theology class in my first year at Bible college. At first I thought the statement was crazy. I thought, *One book? If you read only one book, your mind wouldn't be that open, and God can speak through any book. What's up with this John Wesley guy anyway? There are so many inspirational books out there.* When I finally cooled down enough to understand the context of the quote, I understood what he meant. Wesley was a very well-read guy, but his guide for living rested in God's Word, which is why he said he was a man of one book.

God's Word amazes more and more every day. In it I find promises for everyday living, hope for a bright future, healing when I am in distress and comfort when I am going through a time of sadness. This book rides the roller coaster of life with me and speaks to me through all my highs and lows and everything in between. I am becoming a man of one book. By taking God at His Word, I am understanding this concept more every day. By taking God at His Word, I am learning to trust Him more for all things. God is proving true. He is going above and beyond all that I can ask and think. He is proving Himself over and over again (though He need not do this).

I have started treating the Bible as a conversation with God, and the results have been great. God talks to me through His Word. You must get to know God to make His Word come alive. You will find it fits with whatever you are going through. At certain points in His Word I can hear God yelling at me, and at other times I can hear a faint whisper. I have always liked these couple of verses in Hebrews that talk about the Word.

"For the word of God is alive and powerful. It is sharper than the sharpest two-edged sword, cutting between soul and spirit, between joint and marrow. It exposes our innermost thoughts and desires. Nothing in all creation is hidden from God. Everything is naked and exposed before his eyes, and he is the one to whom we are accountable" (Hebrews 4:12–13 NLT).

If you reflect on these verses you may find that they scare you a bit. They probably should. Two-edged swords are very sharp. The reason they have two edges is so they can get you on the way in or on the way out. Being cut with a two-edged sword would mean certain death in battle, whereas you might survive a blow from a regular sword. The Word of God is sharper than a double-edged sword. It can even separate your soul from your spirit. What's the difference between the two? Your spirit is represented and comes out in your personality, while your soul is the essence of who you are, the deep-down eternal part of you. God's Word separates the two and teaches you the difference. It also exposes your innermost thoughts and desires. These thoughts could be good or bad, but whatever the case, the more you read the Word, the more your soul is exposed. Through your personality, your spirit lives out what your soul desires. Your very essence or being changes as your innermost thoughts and desires are exposed.

The next part of this passage tells us not even to bother trying to hide these things. Sure you can hide them from your friends and your family and live a secret life, but eventually these dark deeds will catch up with you because you can run for only so long. At some point God exposes these things to you in such a way that you simply must deal with them. Eventually the light exposes all. Nothing in creation is hidden from God. Everything is naked and exposed before His eyes, and at some point all of us will be accountable to Him.

Luckily God has designed a way for us to enter His presence with boldness. We have a great high priest in heaven who understands all our shortcomings and pleads to God on our behalf. Because of Christ's work on earth, we now have an advocate in heaven. What a great plan God has for us, and in His Word you can read more about it and how it unfolds for you.

God's Word is alive and powerful. Another translation says it is living and active. I know God's Word is alive because certain passages take on new life each time I read them. I can always glean new meaning each time if I am reading with an open heart and mind and with a desire to know God more. The Holy Spirit gets involved and the words sometimes are bigger on the page or seem to have more inflection. Sometimes I find softer tones in a passage I have previously read.

The Word exposes our innermost thoughts and desires. It causes us to come clean and to be honest with ourselves. It forces us to ask ourselves tough questions. It speaks to our hearts and to our minds. It speaks to us completely. If we read it with an open heart, the Bible brings to the surface who we really are. It convicts us where necessary. It gives us healing words when we need them. It inspires and motivates us for daily living. The Word was meant for us to live out. The Bible teaches us whatever we need to learn. It instructs us on how we should live.

The Bible is the perfect book. If we had only one book to read for the rest of our lives, we wouldn't get bored if we chose the Bible and read it every day until we died.

God, teach me more and more to become a man of one book. Press on...

DEEP SPIRITUAL THOUGHT #871

The Battle

I was reading Revelation 12 and a couple of verses hit me pretty hard. I realized a few things after reading them. The first thing was that I don't spend nearly enough time thinking about or praying in the spiritual realm. I was reminded that a battle is going on in that realm, probably all the time. There is spiritual action all around us. I tend to ignore that part of my faith and choose to focus on other things.

The other realizations came as I was reading verses pertaining to how we defeat Satan and his employees and volunteers. John had a vision of a battle in heaven. Verse 7 says it was a war. Michael and his angels were fighting the dragon and his angels. Verse 10 says the "accuser of our brothers and sisters" was thrown down to earth, and verse 11 says he was "defeated by the blood of the Lamb and by their testimony." It says that "they did not love their lives so much that they were afraid to die." *Their* and *they* refer to the overcoming believers. (These quotes come from the *New Living Translation.*)

These verses tell us how to operate in the spiritual realm, how to deal with the Devil and his angels. We face a battle in our day-to-day living when we are accused by evil, but the blood of the Lamb has already defeated Satan and his angels and booted them out of heaven, though he has been given permission to roam the earth for a period of time. His time is running out. We have been given the formula for victory.

The blood of the Lamb covers all the accusations that Satan may make against us and gives us victory over him. The testimony is the overcomers' word that the Devil has been judged by the Lord. When we sense the Devil's accusations we should verbally testify that Jesus has already dealt with him on the cross. That is the blood of the Lamb the passage mentions. We are to proclaim with our words that our team wins.

We know one of Satan's secrets. He wants to keep this information quiet. He wants as few people as possible to know. He cringes every time someone learns about the dirty little secret that he is trying desperately to protect. The secret is that his future is already clear. This is why he misleads people and tricks people. He is trying to create distraction. But we know the truth: we win every time with the blood of the Lamb and with our testimony.

Satan knows his future, but he doesn't want us to know. We need to tell him that we know. We need to proclaim it by our testimony. That is the second part of the equation and the part we tend to neglect. We often rely solely on the blood of the Lamb and pay little attention to our testimony. But our testimony is how we let Satan know that we know his future. That is how we do battle against the forces of darkness—by the blood of the Lamb (already done) and by our testimony (something we must continually offer).

We need to practice this more if we are to grow deeper into the presence of God. When Satan and his angels start to bug us, we need to proclaim out loud that we know all about their future. We need to say, "Your team loses. Our team wins." Overwhelming victory is ours by the blood of the Lamb and by our testimony. I once saw a T-shirt with this written on it: "The next time Satan reminds you of your past, you remind him of his future." In other words, if he accuses you, confront him with your testimony. Feel free to tell him that you know all about his tricks and his manipulations and his false accusations. Let him know this: "So now there is no condemnation for those who belong to Christ Jesus" (Romans 8:1 NLT).

Tell him you belong to Christ Jesus and no more condemning is allowed. Tell him you know about the abyss and where he is going. It will be one of the best conversations you have had in a long time. Say it out loud because I don't think he is smart enough to hear our thoughts. After all, he is not God. Let him know we win and he loses. Tell him all for the glory of God and for the sake of Jesus and the blood of the Lamb. Thank You, Jesus, for the blood and for the victory, the story that never loses its power.

Press on...

DEEP SPIRITUAL THOUGHT #760

The Greatest of These

It is day 207 of my 365-day journey of seeking and practicing God's presence. I will try to share one of the key lessons I have taken away from this experience. The main point so far has little to do with me. It is mostly about God and His great love and mercy for His people. Unless we experience God's love, nothing we do in this life will matter or have any lasting impact. I know that is a bold statement, but it is the truth. Everything starts with God's love. That and nothing else must be our motivation.

So how do we get that love? How do we experience it? How do we then live it out?

I have learned there is only one way, and that is through the Spirit of God working in and through us. The principle is easy to explain but can seem complicated to live out. I started examining myself against the Bible's definition of love. Immediately I was humbled. I was also a little saddened since many times I seem to fall short in the love department. My instinctive response to problems seems to be anything but loving. That is my human experience. That is why I feel compelled to analyze myself against Scripture from time to time to see how I am doing, and how I can improve. Sometimes I seem to have nothing but love in my heart, and at other times it seems oh so elusive. In those times I need to go back to God's Word to see how I am doing. After examining myself, I allow God's Spirit to help me change the things He wants changed and to improve my performance in the areas where I am starting to do well. But the process starts with the examining. Here is an example that I use.

I seem to gravitate to Corinthians when I struggle in the love department. This verse offers a good beginning: "If I speak in the tongues of men or of angels, but do not have love, I am only a resounding gong or a clanging cymbal" (1 Corinthians 13:1 NIV).

Allow that statement to sink in. The words of the greatest orators known to man are meaningless without love. In fact, their messages become annoying. Gongs and cymbals are loud and irritating after a while and can drive us crazy if we hear them over and over. That is pretty descriptive of how we sound when we talk without being motivated by love. Even if I spoke as eloquently as angels and could get a crowd to do whatever I asked, even if my intentions were good and I was offering my version of God's plan, all this would be meaningless and annoying without love. Love is pretty serious stuff, it would appear.

I am learning that love is an important ingredient as I practice God's presence. To love as God desires is a beautiful thing. Eternity sits up and takes notice. When people are motivated by this kind of love, heaven pays attention.

"If I have the gift of prophecy and can fathom all mysteries and all knowledge, and if I have faith that can move mountains, but do not have love, I am nothing" (1 Corinthians 13:2 NIV). I think Paul is using hyperbole to stress the importance of love. If I could move mountains I would be quite the spectacle. I definitely would have my own reality show. I am not sure how that would play out. Perhaps I would move a mountain an inch to the right and then move it back or for fun put the Rockies in the East for a while. If I could move a mountain, I would be a celebrity. I would probably be known as the greatest illusionist ever because people would think I was performing an illusion. Paul is saying that if I could do that stuff but didn't have love, I would be a nothing. Without love, a talent or a spiritual gift would be meaningless. The type of faith that can move mountains must be accompanied by love for this faith to result in kingdom activity. Paul is saying if I do have that faith, and I have prophetic powers, and I understand all mysteries and possess all knowledge, I can still use all that for evil if it isn't motivated by love.

"If I give all I possess to the poor and give over my body to hardship that I may boast, but do not have love, I gain nothing" (1 Corinthians 13:3 NIV).

The perspective shifts here. Another result of love being lived out is that I become a giver. But if I do not have love and decide to give all I have to the poor so I can brag about it, that too is meaningless.

Why? The answer to this loaded question is found in the following list of love attributes taken from 1 Corinthians 3:4–6 NIV. This is also how I do my personal assessment to see where I fit in this whole love business. Do I have this type of love? Let's find out.

*Love is patient. How am I doing? Not very well. Why did Paul have to start the list off with that one? God help me to be more patient.

*Love is kind. Okay, I am relatively kind. God, help me to be more kind.

*Love does not envy or boast. That is a work in progress for me.

*Love is not arrogant or rude. God, help me to continue to work on my humility.

*Love does not insist on its own way. God, I still struggle with this a little, but I can see improvements, so thank You for working on me and with me in this area.

*Love is not irritable or resentful. It seems I am both of these in varying degrees. God, continue to help me arrive at the kind of love we are talking about so it is evident in both these areas.

*Love does not rejoice at wrongdoing but rejoices with the truth. I do love the truth, so thank You, God, for that.

The NLT translates 1 Corinthians 13:7 in a way that speaks volumes and does not need elaborating. "Love never gives up, never loses faith, is always hopeful, and endures through every circumstance."

Wow! That is quite a checklist. Love never gives up. Do I give up? All these attributes of love raise questions that leave me wondering about myself.

God, help me to learn how to experience the love that comes from You. I know it is too great to understand fully, and that is why I simply need to accept and then experience it. This will lead to fullness of life. That is the goal—fullness of life now and forever. So be it!

"Three things will last forever—faith, hope, and love—and the greatest of these is love" (1 Corinthians 13:13 NLT).

Press on...

Let's Get Physical, and Spiritual

I have been analyzing several areas of my life lately. I tend to do a little inventory every few months. I have been studying physical health and spiritual health and the connections between them. I look back over the past 217 days and I can see that some neat things have happened, but I like to stay intense or else I have a tendency to let stuff slide. I know from experience that letting this happen leads to many things sliding, so I check up on myself.

During the latest inventory I have discovered some things about physical and spiritual fitness that I can improve. Keeping a journal has been a good way to review what I have learned and to see what God has done. A lot of times in these inventories I will ask myself my favorite question: why? I have concluded that I am not in a state of absolute surrender when it comes to my fitness goals. I haven't seemed to reach those tangible goals, so I have to address the why. After observing and reviewing, I have learned that although I have been going to the gym quite regularly, my diet has been inconsistent. At times I have eaten healthy foods, and at times I have eaten fast food. Why can't I be consistent in my diet? That requires a lifestyle commitment. I have to be sold on the idea that diet is 80 percent of the battle while fitness is only about 20 percent rather than vice versa. I realize that I have been only half surrendered to these goals.

Why only half surrendered? Why do I expect full results but go only half stride? Do I really want to reach my fitness and health goals, or am I kidding myself and allowing my subconscious to take over? My subconscious is telling me that if I go to the gym five days a week I can eat whatever I want. Oh, what a tangled web we weave when first we practice to deceive ourselves. Even if I work out five days a week, poor eating will eventually win out over exercise, which will lead to ill health, the opposite of my goal. So what I need to do is get honest with myself and figure out what my real health and fitness goals are.

So what does it mean to be totally surrendered to something? I have come up with an analogy after watching someone ride a bicycle. This person was weaving in and out of traffic. He would turn the handlebars, and the bike would move in the direction he wanted to go. When a car came toward him, he yanked the handlebars the other way, hit the brakes, and did a fancy spin move. The bike was totally under his control. It did exactly what he was asking it to do. He peddled faster and faster and the bike sped up. He arrived at his destination and hit the brakes, and again the bike stopped, surrendering to its master. The man then locked up his bike and entered a store.

This is a great example of something totally surrendered to the will of someone else. The bike was doing what it was created to do, to be surrendered to the person riding it. The bike needs maintenance from time to time, and with that maintenance it will continue to be surrendered for as long as it lasts. The maintenance allows it to function at its best, or to be in absolute surrender mode. If the brakes go and the owner does not get them replaced, when he attempts to brake and the bike doesn't stop, it won't be because the bike doesn't want to be surrendered but because proper maintenance was neglected. If the owner does no maintenance, eventually the bike will not function the way it was meant to function.

We are made in God's image, but sometimes we don't behave as we should, because we forget to do our scheduled maintenance. At times we even become surrendered to ourselves. We spend our time fulfilling our desires. We like to concentrate on our pleasures and to seek possessions that we think will make us happy. At those times our focus is off of God or we are only partially surrendered. Then we behave like the bike with no brakes. It is difficult for us to accept that if we want to be happy we must be totally surrendered to God's will, God's way, God's plan, God's desires for us, God's pleasures. We need to get there with our hearts and our minds. At times we feel this truth in our hearts, but our minds aren't quite sure and vice versa.

We get the concept. We need to be totally surrendered to God's will for our lives. However, we sometimes get tripped up on the application. This is because, just like health and fitness, much discipline is required. I suspect that by nature, we are somewhat lazy, at least a good majority of us. If we aren't lazy, perhaps we focus on the wrong things and keep busy just for the sake of keeping busy. We need daily discipline to check ourselves and to set our goals from the time we get up in the morning to the time we go to bed. If we don't create a plan for our day, then our day will create a plan for us.

Along with discipline, being totally surrendered to God also includes loving His Word and being filled with His love. It's all about being loved and then loving. For the past 217 days I have been seeking this great love. I have been looking to experience what Paul recommends in Ephesians 3:19, and that is the love of Christ, which is too great to understand fully. Paul says that this is what gives me the fullness of life and power that comes from God. My part is to be totally surrendered.

God, help me just for today to be totally surrendered to Your will and to Your way. Help me to be aware of Your presence, because everything good starts with this awareness. Just for today help me to be 100 percent open to where You lead, to what You would have me say and do. Help me to recognize Your love and Your blessings and to be thankful. So be it!

Press on...

DEEP SPIRITUAL THOUGHT #111

Am I Really That Selfish?

Among the greatest enemies of the Christian faith is self. One fruit of the Spirit is love, and God's love is the only thing that can overcome selfishness. Human history shows that self is one of the most consistent hindrances to the faith. It hurts us in our relationship with God and our relationships with others. When we put self first, life gets difficult. Seeking ourselves first is an obstacle to living the abundant life, one lived in the fullness of the Spirit.

The good news is that Christ came to redeem us from this self life. However, the battle against selfishness requires a lot of work on our part, at least at first. The shadow of self follows us around throughout our Christian experience. We must always be aware of this problem and constantly seek God's Spirit and the fruit of that Spirit in our struggle against self. To be delivered from the self life should be a seeker's most consistent prayer. The work that Christ has done has made our deliverance possible. Because of this work, Christ can fill our hearts with His love, leaving less room for the stuff of self.

Being aware of self is the first step. The second step often gets confusing. I sometimes recognize self and immediately act to correct the problem. However, I scratch my head the next time I fail in the same way. I then tend to try harder, and I fall harder still. That seems to be the pattern when I try to fix my self life. It is impossible for me to fix the stuff of self because by nature I am selfish. I tend to become more of the thing I am trying not to be. What is the solution?

I have been praying for God to empty me of all this self stuff so the Holy Spirit can bring fullness to my life. I pray that I will give up control of my thoughts so the Spirit can form them. I pray that I will surrender issues of my heart so the Spirit can lead it. I pray for God to control my hands and my feet so I will be led where He wants me to go. I have been praying to give up total control of my will so that God can bend it the way He wants. My goal is to be wholly His. It's fairly easy to pray for these things but incredibly difficult to practice them. That's because self sneaks in through the back door. I have just kicked him out of the front door, but he is stealthy.

I want to come to God with a heart emptied of all selfish desires. I want to come to Him with a humble heart, one that always puts Jesus first. I want to come to God with a heart open to accepting His plan and willing to take action. That is what I have been praying for, but self trips me up, and I come to God differently than I desire.

How do I really come to God, and how do I tend to pray? "Oh God, please help me with this thing or the other thing," I will pray. "Please heal this person and that person. Please help me with this financial issue. Please bless me in this dealing. Bless my family and take care of them. Please heal me from this or that ailment." O wretched man that I am. Who can save me from myself? God can. The blood of Jesus takes care of all of these self issues. My job is to deny myself, take up my cross, and follow Jesus. This is not a one-time-only deal. I can't make do with having denied myself a bag of chips last June. Scripture says we are to deny ourselves daily. Why daily?

I will answer that question with a question. Jesus seemed to do this all the time, and the technique is a good one. Here is the question. Do you shower every day? Because I get dirty, I shower every day, and this has become part of my routine. The same should be true when dealing with self. We must do this every day and make it a part of our routine.

"Then he said to them all: Whoever wants to be my disciple must deny themselves and take up their cross daily and follow me" (Luke 9:23 NIV).

And that is how we must come to Christ—daily. The good news is that we don't have to do any of the work. God works through us when we have totally surrendered ourselves to His will. Then His Spirit takes over.

"For it is God who works in you to will and to act in order to fulfill his good purpose" (Philippians 2:13 NIV).

Press on...

DEEP SPIRITUAL THOUGHT #471

That's Impossible

I would like to share one of the most significant verses in the Bible, one that has gripped me for years. Two key truths can be drawn from this powerful thought, and I have kept returning to it ever since I have been following Jesus. That's because it encapsulates many other readings along the way. It sums up our faith and how we should live our Christian lives. We must learn these two truths over and over again or at least be reminded of them. That has been my experience in dealing with this verse, which says:

"What is impossible with man is possible with God" (Luke 18:27 NIV).

Don't brush over the two great lessons about the Christian walk that this verse contains. They are imperative for Christian maturity. If I can hold fast to these truths, it means I have finally come to an end of myself and am aware of the resources provided for life through the power of the Holy Spirit. I will at last have become dependent upon God's grace and God's provisions. This is a crucial lesson that I need to learn over and over again.

Does that make me a bad Christian? No, just a human being, so I am strong-willed and stubborn by nature. I was made to fight and to survive. That's why I have an "I've got this" mentality. So the first lesson in this verse takes a long time to learn fully. The lesson is that some things are impossible for man.

There are some things that I cannot do on my own strength and in my own will. That is an extremely difficult lesson to learn and one that I had to revisit repeatedly. I have a learning disability in this area. It is called self. Self wants what self wants, and self will do what self wants to do. We may put a Christian slant on it and say, "Ah, but it is for God. The reason I am doing this is because I believe it will benefit the kingdom. I believe it is God's plan for me. I believe God will bless my ministry. I believe He will be happy with me." But this underscores the first lesson. These statements contain too many references to *I* and *me*. God often calls us to tasks beyond our abilities, and that is the reason we need Him. We need Him because the task is impossible for man

Even the simple task of loving my neighbor, or the even simpler task of loving my brother or sister in Christ, can be impossible. I have discovered that loving others is not that simple and at times requires much grace. At times it seems impossible for man. That is a tough lesson to learn, and sadly some never learn it because love is too much about them. This first lesson is learned only by dying to oneself and surrendering everything to God. We will be ready for the second great lesson of the Christian life only when we finally give up pursuing self-centered carnal stuff. We learn the first lesson only by trying to do things in our own power and failing.

When we fail, we try yet again, saying we will do better this time. But we fail again because we haven't grasped the first lesson. We try many different ways to do what we think God wants us to do, but these attempts are in our own strength and fail even though we pray that God will bless our endeavors for Him. Sadly some people never learn this lesson because of their fighting spirit. We wonder how far we can go and when God will take over. This is all too common in the Christian faith. We know that we have a job to do and that God won't do what we can do, so we try and try again. We think, *Surely if I persevere God will bless my struggles.*

Here is a sobering thought if you haven't learned lesson one. Could it be that you are working from self and that God is not directing you? What if God has a much different plan, but you aren't quiet enough to figure that out? What if you are too busy doing "stuff" for God? I think we all fall into this pattern at some point in our Christian walk. In fact, it is impossible for us to serve God as we were meant to do. It is impossible for us to love the way we are supposed to do. That is because these are spiritual things, and it is impossible for us to do spiritual things in a fleshly manner. We can will to do these things all we want, but it won't change the fact that they are impossible in our own strength. We cannot do these things on our own. We can't will harder or try harder. They are impossible.

Peter is a great example of this. He spent three years hearing Jesus' teachings, but he still didn't get it. He denied Christ three times even though he said he would rather die than do it. That was self talking. His intentions were right, but when Peter acted on his own he denied ever knowing Jesus. That is what self can do. We can talk a good game, but it is impossible for us to follow through in our own strength. Self is strong and stubborn. We want to succeed at whatever we do, and we do not want to back down when we have said something and people have heard us. We have to back up our word and follow through. That is what happens when self is involved. Peter learned this lesson the hard way, and he wound up in tears, indicating repentance.

After he learned the lesson that some things are impossible for man, Peter learned the second lesson: with God, all things are possible. Peter went on to become a Holy Spirit rock star. He got self out of the way and then was open to the Holy Spirit's leading. He became the person whom Jesus told him he would be. Jesus said He would build His church on Peter, but Peter didn't know that this would have nothing to do with self. The stubborn Peter could not perform miracles and be the foundation for the church until he learned these two valuable lessons. Read the book of Acts to see how this played out. Peter underwent an amazing transformation from failing in his own strength to receiving the Holy Spirit and allowing God to work through him. Suddenly everything became possible. God will not give us this Holy Spirit power for work or service if we hold on to self and try to please Him in our own strength. If we are still allowing self to rule, we will not learn this key lesson of Christianity.

This enlightened thinking comes to us as a result of Christian maturity. When I was a new Christian I was a gung-ho-for-Jesus type of guy. I was ready to storm the hill for Christ, so I would try to do stuff for God in my own strength. I would fail, so I would try harder. I would fail again. I had not learned these two invaluable lessons about the Christian life. I seemed to be oblivious to them. Oh, I understood the theory. I knew I needed God to be leading the charge. I knew I had to be filled with the Holy Spirit to have a successful ministry. However, the mind and the heart and the spirit must connect. So I would try and try some more. That led to frustration and to blaming God. *Why, God?* I would wonder. *Why are there not more converts in my ministry? Why aren't there more healings and signs and wonders? I am doing everything right. I am doing this and that. I am, I am, I am.* Yes, I was, and that was the answer to the why. "Your work is not bearing much fruit because you are doing this in your own strength," God might have replied. "I know your intentions are good, but why don't you let Me work through you? Why don't you take Me up on my offer of an easy yoke and a light burden? Why don't you allow Me to will and to act in you according to My good purpose?"

Those questions would haunt me for years until I finally learned the two lessons found in that one verse. I had all the right motivations when I was a young Christian. I was converted, and I had the joy of the Lord in my heart. I was running the race marked out before me (or so I thought). I knew I was in a battle, but I also knew I was on the winning team, and I had all the zeal of a young Christian who was ready to kick some spiritual butt. What could go wrong? At some point in this journey, I realized that what I was attempting to do was impossible in my own strength. However, I didn't accept this reality. Instead I tried harder. There comes a point when you have tried enough times in your own strength and you finally throw up your hands and say *whatever*.

This is a critical point in the battle. You can say, "I have tried and tried and I can't do it, so I will move on to something else," or you can say, "I won't do this on my own anymore. Obviously there is a better way." Your will either move on to lesson two, or you will be beaten up too much by lesson one and give up. This has probably happened to more Christians than we realize. I believe many Christians are living on little faith as a result of beating up themselves. They settle for a life of sin and failure instead of going on to learn lesson two and living a life of rest and victory.

When we finally learn the second lesson that nothing is impossible for God and rest in that truth, then victory comes. Faith is the victory that overcomes the self and the world.

Take time to think about these next questions. What things in your life are seeming impossibilities? What do you suppose God has to say about those impossibilities?

When you finally figure out that doing stuff your way won't work and fully surrender these things to God, then you will see the kind of results that you could only have dreamed about. God will do it! Start allowing God to live His life through you. Then and only then will you be living the abundant life that you were meant to live. And that is only the beginning .

Press on...

DEEP SPIRITUAL THOUGHT #248

Just You Wait a Minute

The greatest failure in my Christian life, and I suspect in many others, is this: I want to work out my faith in part and then ask God to bless it. I need to learn and then to learn some more that "it is God who works in you to will and to act in order to fulfill his good purpose" (Philippians 2:13 NIV). That thought must be engrained in my mind, in my heart, and in my soul. Once I accept Jesus into my life, things change. I need to allow the changes that are led by the Spirit. God has everything planned out. My job is to wait on Him.

And there is where I fall apart. This is such a good theory, but I have to do what? My role is to wait on the Lord? That seems easy. The problem comes when I want to work out my faith on my own and ask God to bless what I am doing. It comes when I insist on my interpretation of what God thinks and ask Him to join me in what I am doing. I pray fervently that God will bless my interpretation of what He wants for me. So what seems simple on the surface is suddenly complicated by self, and self interprets everything in life a little differently than the Holy Spirit does. So what do I do? Wait on the Lord.

I am definitely no expert on the idea, but I have learned a thing or two about waiting on the Lord. I have waited in different ways, depending on my walk of faith. When I was asked to leave my ministry position because of family issues, I waited on God in a way that amounted to questioning what exactly was going on. The only thing I could do was wait on the Lord. That waiting, however, was not the kind that I advocate. It was tinged by the pain I was going through. After a few years of this kind of waiting, I began another kind.

At first I felt I'd had the carpet pulled from under my feet and wondered would happen next. Then I settled into an apathetic kind of waiting. This kind is the most dangerous. You throw up your hands and say, "I have been waiting on God for a long time now, and it seems like nothing is happening. I will continue to wait on God but live life based on my own agenda." That is the opposite of accepting that "it is God who works in you to will and to act in order to fulfill his good purpose." My version was, "It is Trevor who works in Trevor to will and then to act that out according to the purposes of Trevor." At this stage, I was blind to God's purpose for me, and the longer I remained in this situation the further I wandered from that purpose.

A few years go by and another form of waiting begins. God arranges events in our lives that convince us to give up what we want, and He helps us once again to see His purpose for us. This next type of waiting on God comes in the form of healing and restoration. We now know that we cannot possibly do the stuff of God on our own, so we accept this type of waiting with open arms. We want to wait on God and let Him guide us, because we have usually come to the end of ourselves and realize that God always wanted the best for us. We recognize that we were too wrapped up in our own vision of what God wanted for us to see His plan. So we wait with faith. Our faith grows in this type of waiting. The fires of the Holy Spirit are reignited from deep within. We learn so much in this phase, including what it means to listen to God and to accept His leading. We learn how to wait on God. We realize that God is at work within us, giving us the will to serve Him, and we know that He will do the work through us. This is a great growth phase.

In the next form of waiting, I have learned that waiting for the sake of waiting will get me nowhere. I have learned that waiting anxiously is not good either. When I am waiting anxiously, I look for signs from God everywhere, and I am ready to jump the gun on what I think He wants. I have to take care that I do not fall back into doing things my way as I did when my faith was immature. Faith is above feeling, but on some days I feel I should be involved in this or in that. However, instead of jumping, I wait on the Lord. He then makes it clear what direction I should take. God has been speaking loud and clear, and I have known beyond a shadow of a doubt that all my decisions as of late are from Him. That is a great place to be. Trusting God totally is the right way to wait.

I now enjoy a resting type of waiting. That is what the Bible means when it talks about waiting. I am learning how to wait on the Lord. I am trusting Him completely with every area of my life—my family, my health, my career, and my calling. I am totally open to His leading, and I am learning how to live at rest each day. Philippians 2:13 has taken on a much different meaning. It is God who works in me to will, and I know that He is giving me the desire to become more like Jesus. God works in me to give me the desire to serve Him, and He also puts it into action through me. My job is to be obedient and to wait in rest on the Lord day by day.

Waiting now means I am resting in God's presence. I am aware of His presence, and every decision I make now incorporates it. I still have a tendency to jump the gun, but I remember to rest in the waiting. Doing that provides spiritual power. How long do I have to wait? It doesn't matter, because waiting on the Lord has become a way of life. It has become my new way of living the spiritual life. It is the overcomer's life, the more-than-a-conqueror's life. It is the Christ-like life that God wants to live through us.

When you trust God totally, you have faith in His time line, and if you have to wait a day, a week, a month, a year, or even a decade, your waiting is never in vain. This type of waiting also gives you much-increased growth in faith. When you rest in your waiting, God grows your faith. You begin to see how everything works together for the good according to His plan.

That is victory-filled waiting.

"Wait for the Lord; be strong and take heart and wait for the Lord" (Psalm 27:14 NIV).

Press on...

Holy Flow!

It is shocking how much we can and will do in our own strength. We can live our Christian lives, get involved in Christian service, run our ministries, lead our families, juggle our careers, and everything else in between with our own strength. We can do all these things in our own power. But oh how futile these things are or can become.

What should we do about this? We are strong-willed, stubborn people who love our independence and take pride in the fact that we can do things on our own. I know how that side of life works. I know the emptiness and the meaninglessness that my own efforts produce. I know how little inspiration or power to change the world come as a result of these efforts.

What I want to learn most in the second half of my life is total dependence on the Holy Spirit, not just in word but in action. I want to live my life out of the power that results from knowing God and spending time in His presence. I want to be so in tune with God's Spirit that every decision and every action are led by the Holy Spirit and not by good-intentioned Trevor. I am willing to yield every area of my life to Christ's leading.

However, I still wrestle with the flesh and the many ways it is manifested. I like to think I am a fairly intelligent person, so I manifest fleshly wisdom that sounds just spiritual enough. I may even share some of that wisdom with a friend, or by writing, or in front of a small group. I may be busy with things of the church and of God's kingdom, and yet the power of the Holy Spirit may be absent from that wisdom and from that service. Perhaps that is why there is lots of kingdom work going on but the results may be a little lackluster. When the Holy Spirit is absent, the work is futile. I understand this type of service because I know it is easy to get caught up in being busy for God. The tendency is to say, "Hey, I'm smart. I can read what the Bible says, and I can tell others about it. No problem." There is a problem, though, and it is called religious self-effort. I am guilty of this when I take it upon myself to do the work of the Holy Spirit. How silly that is. Only the Holy Spirit can do the work of the Holy Spirit.

I want to live the second half of my life in this holy flow. I want to live in such a way that it is no longer I who lives but Christ who lives in me. I want to give up my wants and my thoughts about how life should go and live instead in the holy flow. I want to know what the holy flow wants me to know and to go where it takes me. The way to enter this holy flow is by giving God my undivided attention, my full surrender. It would be enough for me to rest in this holy flow, but I know that the Word calls me to more.

That is where the dilemma enters and I sometimes get caught up in doing things my way. The Word tells me to go and make disciples of all nations. How do I do that? What percentage of the task falls to me? The Word also instructs me to take part in good works that were prepared in advance for me to do. Where do I find these good works? Do I look for them? How do I get into this holy flow so I am not looking for all these things to do and for people so I can make them disciples?

Thank You, God, that I do not have to stress over these things anymore. Thank You that I do not have to do things in my own flesh. Thank You for providing the perfect plan, which is to get to know You more. That's it? That's it!

I finally understand that the plan relies completely on knowing God's rest. I have known that in theory for many years, but thanks be to God I now understand it with my heart. Working in the flesh produces complete frustration that leads down many fruitless paths. Resting in the One who tells us His yoke is easy and His burden light is the only way to enter that holy flow and to stay there. At this point we start to live out the truth that it is God who works in us to will and to act according to His good purpose.

Thank You, God, that You have already worked this out and that I can finally stop doing things in my own strength and in my own stubbornness. May I forever live in Your holy flow. My prayer for all who read this is that they may also know the peace that is theirs when they submit themselves to Your holy flow.

Press on...

DEEP SPIRITUAL THOUGHT #187

Spiritual Invincibility

As I was on a prayer walk this morning, a neat thought entered my mind. It seems that the closer I get to Jesus, the more I get to know God and learn how to practice His presence, and when I allow His Holy Spirit to run my life, I come closer to spiritual invincibility. I know I am only human, and my body is vulnerable, but spiritual invincibility is altogether different.

I can do all things through Christ who strengthens me, because it is no longer I who lives but Christ who lives in me, and that is as close to spiritual invincibility as any of us will ever get.

When we are at spiritual meetings, conventions, camps, or other places with many people and inspired worship, it is somewhat easy to have a mountaintop experience with Jesus. During worship, inspirational speeches, enlightened times of prayer, or moments alone with God when we sense His presence, we feel invincible spiritually. We feel that we can do all things through Christ who strengthens us, because we believe Jesus is living His life through us and it is no longer we who live. Why do we feel that way in those times? I think it is because we allow our minds and our hearts to believe that impossibilities are possible when we are immersed in God's presence.

What about when we are feeling down or we have just received terrible news about our health or about a family member? Why do we not approach life with the same feeling of invincibility then? What if we could take those thoughts of invincibility into our everyday lives? What do you suppose might happen? I believe we can have that feeling of invincibility even in our darkest hour. When we allow God to renew our minds, we can get to the stage where we believe we can do all things through Christ.

How do we renew our minds? There is a hint of this in Paul's letter to the Romans. "Therefore, I urge you, brothers and sisters, in view of God's mercy, to offer your bodies as a living sacrifice, holy and pleasing to God—this is your true and proper worship. Do not conform to the pattern of this world, but be transformed by the renewing of your mind. Then you will be able to test and approve what God's will is—his good, pleasing and perfect will" (Romans 12:1–2 NIV).

So how do we have our minds renewed so as to attain spiritual invincibility? Simply by offering God our bodies as a living sacrifice and by refusing to conform to the pattern of this world. I like reading this in *The Message*. Eugene Peterson has a great translation of these verses. He writes the passage this way:

> So here's what I want you to do, God helping you: take your everyday, ordinary life—your sleeping, eating, going-to-work, and walking-around life—and place it before God as an offering. Embracing what God does for you is the best thing you can do for him. Don't become so well-adjusted to your culture that you fit into it without even thinking. Instead, fix your attention on God. You'll be changed from the inside out, and quickly respond to it. Unlike the culture around you, always dragging you down to its level of immaturity, God brings the best out of you, develops well-formed maturity in you. (Romans 12:1–2 MSG)

Stop allowing the things of the world to reduce you to their level. That is a great piece of advice for gaining spiritual invincibility. The world will try to bring you down from the spiritual highs you are on after a camp meeting, a convention, or a worship service. If you want to mature in your faith and grow closer to God by living like Jesus did, you must see the world for what it is and not fall for its glitter or succumb to its sneak attacks.

So how do we get along in the world? How do we make a difference for Christ among nonbelievers if we aren't in this world? We are supposed to be in this world but not of it. When we offer God our ordinary lives, our sleeping, eating, going-to-work, and walking-around lives, we are changed, and we know the meaning of being in the world but not of the world. We don't fall into the trap of being too heavenly minded to do any earthly good, but we don't flirt with the world either. We simply give every part of our lives to God: the spiritual highs, the normal walking-around days, and the devastating low times. When we learn to embrace what God is doing for us, we can fix our attention on Him. We will be changed from the inside out, and that is a promise we can take to the bank. When this happens, God will bring out the best in us and allow us to mature spiritually. Then we will be well on our way to spiritual invincibility.

My goal is to have the same belief in God when I am on top of the world, when I am going about my everyday life, and when I am devastated by bad news. I know that in all ways and at all times I can do all things through Christ who strengthens me, because it is no longer I who lives but Christ who lives in me.

Press on (to spiritual invincibility).

DEEP SPIRITUAL THOUGHT #341

Can I Get Some Help?

I woke up this morning with a couple of questions on my mind. *Where does my help actually come from?* I wondered. It is trite to say, "My help comes from above" or "My help comes from God." The real question is, do I believe this? Also, are there degrees of belief? Where does my help come from when my level of concern goes up or when my problems get bigger? Where does my help come from when my problems seem unbearable? When it seems like life is getting too tough, does my help come from the same place? Or will I start to think, *Perhaps there is no help?* When I was satisfied with my answer to the question about the source of my help, I wondered, *Where does my fulfillment come from?* I came to a few conclusions, at least for me.

The answer to my questions, I concluded, was that I gain help and fulfillment by living in the presence of Jesus through the Holy Spirit. As I considered how I can live in Christ's presence, I recalled that God's Word says Jesus is closer to me than breathing. Think about that for a second. What is closer than breathing? Try breathing for a second. What happened? You will notice that nothing much happened. Now try taking a deep breath, and as you do, think about something good that Jesus represents to you. That will change the way you breathe.

I then thought, *How can Jesus be closer to me than breathing?* I concluded that the only way this was possible was by living His life through me. If I allow Him total control, I find that He moves my feet and my hands, and I end up in places led by Him, at times ordained by Him. The more I get to know Jesus, the more I get to know me. More important, the more I get to know Jesus, the more I become like the person I think I should be, like the picture I have of myself as a follower of Christ. As I look at this picture, I realize that I am changing.

I am moving slowly from one degree of glory to another, and that is an exciting change. This is not happening by my own strength or by my own will but by the Spirit of God that is alive within me. God can do immeasurably more than all I could imagine. He does more than I could ever ask, according to that power that is at work within me. That is resurrection power. The same power that raised Jesus from the grave is now within me, making me more like Jesus, allowing me to change slowly but surely, one degree of glory at a time. There is no greater plan in all of the universe than Jesus alive in me, closer than the breath I take. Wow! Thank You, Jesus, that You know me and that You are alive in me.

The road is long, and there is much work to do. The hardest part of the journey is staying in God's presence. Once we get that part figured out, we can accomplish the work we must do through the Spirit moving us and guiding us. We have to keep pressing on in faith, but when we do our job, God keeps us in His grace. He works in us to will and to act according to His good purpose. We need to learn this key lesson of the faith, relearn it, practice it, and then learn it some more until it becomes a part of who we are. Then one day we will come to the awareness that Jesus is closer to us than breathing. How cool is that?

The Bible tells us this experience is above all that we can ask or think. To reach this point, we must be alone with God and understand His omnipotence. We must recognize whom we are dealing with. God is all-powerful, all-knowing, outside space and time, and can do much more than we can ever imagine. Knowing this is only the first step. Once we learn about God's omnipotence, we must trust in that omnipotence. Imagine trusting in someone who knows everything there is to know about everything, has all the power there is to have, and is not constrained by space and time. Once we come to that realization, we are living up to our Christian name. That is the knowledge Jesus had and the power that He relied upon while in His human form. That same power is now available for those of us who will believe and trust.

This is the life the Christian was meant to live—a life of fullness, a life spent loving God and those who were created in His image. How much time have I wasted while not trusting in God's omnipotence? How much time have I wasted trusting in my own strength? A Christian living a full life loves and waits on God and trusts Him no matter what. We cannot do God's will except by the power of God. He gives us the first experience of His power when we accept Him for salvation. He gives us just enough to long for more. He wants us to grow into the people we are meant to become, people full of Holy Spirit power, people who put their total trust in Him.

Once we have put our total trust in Him, He becomes closer to us than breathing, and we can live the life that He has prepared for us.

"I lift up my eyes to the mountains—where does my help come from? My help comes from the Lord, the maker of heaven and earth" (Psalm 121:1–2 NIV).

Press on...

DEEP SPIRITUAL THOUGHT #924

Keeping Power

> The Lord will keep you from all evil—he will
> watch over your life; the Lord will watch over your
> coming and going both now and forevermore.
> —Psalm 121:7–8 NIV

There it is again, that keeping power. Staying on the right path
through the highs and the lows of life can be hard. It can be tough
to remain in God's presence when you get news that knocks the
wind out of you or when you see an iceberg glistening up ahead
in the bay. That's why keeping power may be one of the most
important of God's abilities.

After we are born again and become Christians, believing in
the Lord Jesus Christ for salvation, we quickly grow in grace. At
first the experience is exciting because it is new, but because we
live in a society suffering from acute attention-deficit disorder,
we tend to get bored. When we get bored in our faith we enter
the danger zone and may start to drift away. There is no sense in
blaming God, because the fault lies with us.

If we draw near to God, He will draw near to us. That is a
promise. If we resist the devil, he will flee. The Lord will keep
you from all evil, as the psalm says. We only need to resist and
then God will take over. But we do need to resist. That is our

part. God does the rest. When we stop drawing near to God due to boredom or spiritual lethargy, He won't draw near to us, and we suffer. We tend to drift away spiritually. Understanding that God is the one who keeps us is crucial. We must come to God with a humble, open, and willing heart. Then He will work in us to will and to do according to His good purpose. We must to submit to His will every day and come into His presence. The more we do that and the nearer we draw to God, the nearer He draws to us. That is the way all intimate relationships work. The closer we draw to our loved ones, the closer they draw to us.

So what is this keeping power all about? What does the psalm mean when it says the Lord will keep "your going out and your coming in"? This is where the keeping power kicks in. When we are kept in God's grace we have a choice to make. We can keep learning more, or we can drift away. We can advance to spiritual maturity, or we can do nothing and stay on the spiritual bottle. Again we have a role to play. God's keeping power comes into play when we pursue spiritual growth. Our task is to grow in the grace and knowledge of our Lord and Savior Jesus Christ. We should take God at His word and put aside doubt. (We all tend to doubt, but we shouldn't get caught up in this pitfall.) We must claim a promise over a problem and allow God's Spirit to work in us. That is keeping power.

The keeping power of God is meant to be continuous. When we break fellowship with God, we have to figure out where and when this happened, repent, and move on. Life is continuous and our relationship with God must be the same way. His gifts and promises are permanent. God's life is lived out through His church, or *ecclesia* in the Greek, meaning "the called-out people of God."

So God's life is lived through us individually, and together we form the body. God offers to be our keeper, and He watches over us day by day, hour by hour, crisis by crisis. This in no way means we will be in a perpetual state of happiness, but it does mean that God will make His power available to us every moment of every day to give us victory over darkness, sadness, sickness, and all of life's other travails. He gives us the power to get through one day at a time. He gives us the power to live in the mundane and to find things there to be thankful for. He is with us and leads us to the mountaintops to show us what could be. During these experiences, He reveals a little of His glory and what He has in store for us. He gives us everything we need to live the life that He has prepared for us.

Can God keep me in His presence for one day? I think we would all agree that this is possible. There have been days when God has kept my heart in His presence, even though my flesh and sinful nature were struggling to come out and play. He has kept me from all that could go wrong in one day. So it is possible to be kept from sin for a day. Well, if one day is possible, what about two? No problem. My goal is to measure my expectations against God's Word and to claim His promises as mine.

Here is an irony. God is constantly speaking to us through His Word, but we sit back, looking befuddled, and say, "If only I could hear from God. Why can't I hear from Him?" I think this must tick Him off a bit. We are showing how little we understand about the holy, omnipotent God we serve. I know I am guilty of this. God has promised that He will keep us by His great power, that He will protect us from all evil and will guard our lives. That promise is for us if we believe His Word. Our part is to say, "Okay, God, I accept Your promise. Keep me from all evil, from fear, from sickness, from danger. Keep me aware of all the tricks of the Enemy. Keep me in Your love, in Your grace, in Your peace, in Your joy. Keep me faithful, and keep me patient as I wait for You. Keep me from growing weary as I wait to hear from heaven. Keep me in Your presence. God, keep me!" Our spiritual life and the works of service that flow from our faith are God's doing. He works in us to will and to do according to His good purpose.

When we finally come to the point in our spiritual lives where we accept that truth by faith, God will work in us and through us. To think that I have been trying to please Him by starting or leading ministries in my own strength and according to my own agenda. How presumptuous to believe that I knew what God wanted and that I could take it from there! I certainly understand the sin of presumption. I have presumed to know the mind of God, putting His label on my ideas for ministry.

God, I want You to walk ahead of me and prepare the way. I want to be filled with Your keeping power day in and day out. Thank You for filling me with this power day in and day out. I accept it. Thank You for making all things beautiful in Your time. Jesus, keep me forever in Your presence. So be it!

Press on...

DEEP SPIRITUAL THOUGHT #763

Sanctification

This is a pretty deep topic, so instead of trying to describe exactly what sanctification is, I will share some thoughts I had about it as I was crying out to God. The thoughts flowed from a question: how can I learn the secret to the spiritual life? The starting point to learning this secret is utter helplessness—not helplessness as in being no good for anything, but spiritual helplessness. I experience this when I finally come to the end of myself, my own ideas, my own strength, my own abilities, and come to God in complete and utter humility. Then the door to spiritual reality opens, and if I enter, my learning is greatly and speedily enhanced.

I gave up everything I was holding on to and prayed that God would show me other things that I might be holding on to without realizing it. I finally saw that it was impossible for me to live the holy life, the set apart life, the sanctified life, on my own. I started allowing God to live His life through me. I began taking the Bible to heart and believing God's Word as if He were talking to me. In fact, He was! That is when changes began. I had to learn how to trust God fully, a tough lesson. We hear about it from preachers all the time, but we often fail miserably when it comes to allowing God to live His life through us. Trusting God fully is difficult. It means I must completely die to my own ideas about what I should be doing or how I should be living. Trust comes only through the death of self, which is the beginning of sanctification (or being set apart fully for God). I had to learn through the school of hard knocks exactly what that meant. Unfortunately, I was stubborn, so I learned a little more slowly. I couldn't simply listen to someone tell me. I had to learn everything the hard way.

That was then. Now I am more open to what I hear from other people, because I have had the stubbornness knocked out of me. Now I can listen to what someone has to say and learn from that person. The same is true when I hear from God. I listen. Sometimes I am still a little slow, but I guess I am making sure that God is speaking and that the idea is not mine.

I was recently reading 1 Corinthians 1, and a lightbulb came on regarding sanctification. Theologically speaking, the term can be batted around all day with little spiritual benefit. I know this from experience. In my college days we talked extensively about sanctification to the point of beating the topic to death. Sanctification is now something I would rather live than debate. So what did I learn from 1 Corinthians 1? So much is packed into this chapter that I suggest making it your devotional for the next three days and allowing God to speak to you about it.

This chapter focuses on our relationship to Jesus. Paul makes it quite clear who Jesus is and who we are. He starts by telling us that we are united with Jesus. He then talks about the grace that God has made available to us through Jesus. Every aspect of our lives can be enriched with this grace. This is a great point. Some of us think, *Sure God can help me with this problem, but there is no way He can help me in this area. I am too far gone there.* Paul says the opposite. Verse 5 puts it like this: "In this grace, God is enriching every aspect of your lives by gifting you with the right words to say and everything you need to know." Verses 6 and 7 add emphasis, saying, "In this way, your life story confirms the life story of the Anointed One, so you are not ill-equipped or slighted on any necessary gifts as you patiently anticipate the day when the Lord Jesus, the Anointed One, is revealed." And what do we do as we await that day? Verse 8 says, "Until that final day, He will preserve you, and on that day, He will consider you faultless" (1 Corinthians 1:5–8, The Voice). Imagine me faultless.

This is the real deal. Another translation says we are partners with Jesus. God did this through His amazing grace. With sanctification we can live the same life that Jesus lived, not as imitators but as people who have been given the Spirit that was in Jesus, making us partners in faith. In fact, all who are set apart for Christ are partners. (The word *sanctification* means "being set apart.") When we say *brothers and sisters in Christ*, we could also say *partners*. If we are partners with someone in business, we typically have the same values and the same mission. That is also how it is with the community of Christ. We have all received from Christ.

There is a great mystery in this whole business of sanctification. The mystery is Christ in me. All the characteristics that made Jesus who He was are given to me when I have faith enough to receive them or after I have been through the school of hard knocks and have finally come to the end of myself. This is mind-boggling. With sanctification, the holiness of Jesus becomes mine. I allow Jesus to take over my fleshly life, which is always in battle with the spirit. Jesus now takes first place in my flesh and in my spirit, and I receive His holy qualities. I receive His love, joy, peace, patience, goodness, faithfulness, kindness, gentleness, and self-control.

I know that Jesus Christ was the only perfect human being, and now, through sanctification, I receive all those perfections. This becomes a lifelong growing experience. That is why songs like "The Longer I Serve Him the Sweeter He Grows" make so much sense. God is not changing, but I am, growing slowly but surely in sanctification, moving from one degree of glory to another, all because of what Jesus did. "Therefore, as the Scriptures say, 'If you want to boast, boast only about the Lord'" (1 Corinthians 1:31 NLT).

Press on to the sweetness of sanctification.

DEEP SPIRITUAL THOUGHT #054

When You Have Nothing to Say

> For the mouth speaks what the heart is full of.
> —Matthew 12:34 NIV

What comes out of your heart when you seemingly have nothing to say? In the first part of Matthew 12, Jesus is lambasting the Pharisees and trying to teach them the truth. They are having none of it and even call Him Satan and say He is demon-possessed. In verse 34 Jesus calls them a brood of snakes and asks how evil men like them could speak what is good and right. Then He tells them that what is in their hearts determines what they will say. Out of the overflow of the heart the mouth speaks. Wow!

What are we putting in our hearts? What do we hold in our hearts in such a quantity that it spills out of us? Love? Joy? Peace? Or anger, jealousy, bitterness, and other ugly stuff? We all must answer this question for ourselves. Or we can ignore it, stay on spiritual automatic pilot, fail to examine ourselves, and remain oblivious to what goes into our hearts. We can live our lives the same old way and pretend that everything is good. That is one approach.

When I began this journey of practicing God's presence, I started examining everything that I put into my heart and my mind, because I knew that what goes in will at some point come out. So what did I want to come out? If I wanted love, joy, peace, patience, kindness, goodness, gentleness, faithfulness, and self-control to emanate from my being, then that is what I needed to feed my heart and my mind. I decided to start with God's Word. I wanted to insert the Bible into my conscious and subconscious mind. If I could have done it, I would have hooked myself up to an IV to take in God's Word. However, I needed to do the hard work of reading and reflecting on Scripture. I had to devote time to the Word in order for the outflow of my mouth to be pleasing to God. If I were stranded on a desert island and had only one book with me, I pray it would be the Bible.

This verse talks about the things we take to heart. A friend of mine loves comedy. He eats, sleeps, and listens to comedy. He memorizes the bits so he can share them with his friends. It is easy to see what the overflow of his heart is. Comedy enters his mind, goes through his heart, and then comes out of his mouth. That is true with anything. We put stuff in our minds that filters through our hearts and eventually comes out of our mouths. Did you ever say something and later admit that you didn't know where it came from? It came from something you put in your heart at some point that emerged with the overflow.

It is my responsibility to check what goes into my heart. I am responsible for what comes out of my mouth. I choose to put the things of God into my heart. A year ago, I chose to spend time with God simply by being in His presence. For 365 days I wanted to do an experiment to practice God's presence and see what the results would be. Do I still have struggles? Absolutely. But I notice that my bounce-back time is quick. I no longer dwell on the negative. I still think bad thoughts and struggle with fleshly stuff, but I immediately pray or start thinking about things of God, and I don't stay in the negative space for long. I used to like having pity parties. I think that is human nature. "Oh, look at poor me. This happened to me, and now I am going to feel bad for a few days. I deserve to be negative and to have a pity party."

Things enter the heart, sit there for a while, and eventually come out of your mouth, sometimes when you least expect it.

Here is a personal example. I just returned from an excellent trip to the East Coast. My wife and I, along with our three kids, had an amazing time taking in the beauty of Atlantic Canada. I saw some sights that I am sure are as lovely as any on earth. God showed me a whole new level of His beauty because I was in His presence. My heart overflowed with the beauty of God's earth. As a part of that overflow, I put many pictures of my trip on the Internet for my friends to see. I wanted to share God's handiwork with everyone who was willing to look, because I know that many people appreciate the beauty of nature.

On the fifth day of our trip as we were driving by a beautiful landscape in Summerside, Prince Edward Island, I got a call from my doctor's office. I had some blood work done before I left for my trip, and the doctor told me that he thought I had some kind of lymphoma cancer and that I needed to see an oncologist as soon as I returned. Here is the beauty in that story: God had just brought me through a year of practicing His presence, and my first thought upon hearing the news was, *God's got this. Whatever this is, I know that God is in control and that whatever happens will be for His glory.* Before my year of practicing His presence, I would have been bitter and angry at God and yelled and screamed at Him, because the overflow of my heart would have been bitterness. A bitter root would have taken hold, and I would have been in a dark place for a long time.

Thank God that was not the case. The overflow of my heart now tells a different story. God is so good, and I thank Him for all He is doing, for all He has done, and for what He will do. I know for sure that this story is far from over. Stay tuned (and if you think about it, pray for me). And no, this news did not ruin my trip. In fact it intensified my appreciation for life and for God's artwork.

Press on...

DEEP SPIRITUAL THOUGHT #119

The Great Mystery

I love a great mystery. It engages my senses and intrigues my mind. I was reminded recently of a great mystery. I love trying to solve a mystery Hardy Boys style, or perhaps Scooby Doo style. I love running all the scenarios through my mind. My family and I will watch a mystery and come up with all sorts of diabolical scenarios that the writers didn't even consider. In the end, I find the answers to the mystery are usually pretty easy. It is usually something as simple as "The butler did it." Yep, should have known all along. It's always the butler.

I was reading Colossians and got a simple reminder to keep me on track with my lifestyle choice of drawing nearer to God so that He would draw nearer to me. In these verses Paul talks about a mystery, probably the greatest ever—the mystery of the gospel. But he gives us a simple explanation, kind of like saying the butler did it. Paul begins by explaining his commission.

> I have become its servant [the church's] by the commission God gave me to present to you the word of God in its fullness—the mystery that has been kept hidden for ages and generations, but is now disclosed to the Lord's people. To them God has chosen to make known among the Gentiles the glorious riches

of this mystery, which is Christ in you, the hope of glory. He is the one we proclaim, admonishing and teaching everyone with all wisdom, so that we may present everyone fully mature in Christ. To this end I strenuously contend with all the energy Christ so powerfully works in me. (Colossians 1:25–29 NIV)

The solution to the mystery in a nutshell is this: Christ is in you, the hope of glory, for the purpose of spiritual maturity. That is it. The mystery is solved. Paul says that is the substance of our message as Christians. "We preach Christ, warning people not to add to the Message. We teach in the spirit of profound common sense so that we can bring each person to maturity. To be mature is to be basic. Christ! No more, no less. That's what I'm working so hard at day after day, year after year, doing my best with the energy God so generously gives me" (Colossians 1:28–29 MSG).

That says it all for me. Jesus is alive in me, the hope of glory. I don't have to struggle with the stuff of self, though I still do. That's mysterious. Christ lives in me when I allow Him to and solves that mystery. I need to come to Him every day, deny myself, and take up my cross. Then He comes and lives in me, and it is no longer I who live but Christ who lives in me. Mystery solved: Christ in me. The stuff that I used to deem impossible is suddenly possible because Christ is living in me, and with God impossibilities become possibilities. I can now do things that were seemingly impossible before this mystery was revealed—things like living a holy life and loving the way God taught me to love. What seemed so much more than I could ever ask or imagine also enters the realm of possibility because Christ is in me.

Paul said he was working hard at preaching Christ, no more and no less. He said he was doing his best with the energy God so generously gave him. So what am I doing with the energy that God so generously gives me? This is a tough question for me, since I do not have a lot of energy these days. I fear that I wasted a lot of my energy before on things that didn't matter. I need to spend more time on the things of Christ. I need to meditate more on the truth that is Christ in me, the hope of glory, and use whatever energy God gives me wisely both now and in the future.

That is my prayer: Christ in me, living out the life He wants to live through me, which is the hope of glory. Mystery solved.

Press on...

Jesus Is Coming

Jesus is coming! The apostle Paul's had an amazing urgency about the things of the Lord and wrote as if He were coming back any day now. So I asked myself some questions in my reflection time. Did Paul really believe Jesus was returning soon, or was he saying this to underscore his message because he knew people were procrastinators by nature? Do I live my life as if Jesus could come back any day? Do I approach life with that same urgency? Sadly and clearly, I do not. So I had to dig a little deeper and ask why.

Paul's writings make clear that he wanted people to come to know Christ right away. Procrastination was not part of his makeup. Having Ghad several face-to-face encounters with Jesus, he was perhaps anxious that others get to know the Lord ASAP. Paul knew human beings and was a master at dealing with people. He could debate with religious leaders, preach to the common folk, converse with scholars and poets, and even testify in front of kings. He had no fear of talking about Jesus. I believe this was because he had met Him. I can't even imagine what that would be like. At times I have felt close to God and have heard from Him, but I have never seen Him face to face. Think of the times when you have felt closest to God. In those moments you had no fear of being bold for Jesus. That seems to be how Paul operated all the time. To do this requires practice in God's presence and urgency about His Word.

I have been returning to Philippians more and more and was recently struck by this passage: "Do not be anxious about anything, but in every situation, by prayer and petition, with thanksgiving, present your requests to God. And the peace of God, which transcends all understanding, will guard your hearts and your minds in Christ Jesus" (Philippians 4:6–7 NIV).

Do not be anxious about anything? Does Paul mean do not be anxious when I have no money and the rent is due? Does he mean do not be anxious when I have a big test tomorrow that will determine my future? Does he mean do not be anxious when I was in an accident and wrecked my new car? Does he mean do not be anxious when I got laid off from work and I am now unemployed? Does he mean do not be anxious when I didn't get into the school I wanted to attend? Does he mean do not be anxious when I just got diagnosed with a terrible disease?

Apparently, the answer to all of these questions is yes. That is how faith-filled Paul was. Okay, if he has such outrageous expectations, he must tell us how we go about doing this, right? The passage says that in every situation we should present our requests to God through prayer and petition. If we do these things, the peace of God, which transcends all understanding, becomes ours.

If this makes no sense and you think there is no way you can have peace in the scenarios mentioned above, then you get it. You cannot understand this promise or have this peace on your own. The peace Paul describes is a supernatural gift. The peace of God will guard your heart and your mind in Christ Jesus. So not only do you get this supernatural peace, but you get divine protection.

You do this by rejoicing always, as Paul says in Philippians 4:4. Even when you are in terrible situations, you are to rejoice. When he wrote this he was staring at a cement wall in a cold, dark jail cell. In verse 5, Paul explains the reason to rejoice: the Lord is near. He alone can grant the gift of supernatural peace.

I like how Paul ties this up by telling us how to keep our hearts and our minds guarded in Christ Jesus.

"Finally brothers and sisters, whatever is true, whatever is noble, whatever is pure, whatever is lovely, whatever is admirable—if anything is excellent or praiseworthy—think about such things. Whatever you have learned or received or heard from me, or seen in me— put it into practice. And the God of peace will be with you" (Philippians 4:8–9 NIV).

The God of peace will be with us when we set our minds on those things.

I love the way *The Message* translates Philippians 4:4–5 as it deals again with the urgency that we are talking about. The *New International Version* translates verse 5 as "The Lord is near." Here is now *The Message* reads.

"Celebrate God all day, every day. I mean, revel in him! Make it as clear as you can to all you meet that you're on their side, working with them and not against them. Help them see that the Master is about to arrive. He could show up any minute!" (Philippians 4:4–5 MSG).

What do you suppose would happen if we believed that? Today we hardly even think about it. But Jesus is coming and maybe very soon. That should change the way we think, which will lead us to change our actions. I will think about such things.

Press on...

DEEP SPIRITUAL THOUGHT #423

Thanks

The Psalms talk a lot about giving thanks. "Give thanks to the Lord, for He is good; His love endures forever" (Psalm 107:1 NIV).

Give thanks with a grateful heart. Give thanks to the Holy One. Give thanks because He's given us Jesus Christ, His Son. That alone should be more than enough reason to give thanks. If we gave God thanks just for this one thing, it would be more than enough to fill up a lifetime, at least if we were doing this as He deserves. However, we tend to fall short in the gratitude department from time to time. If we thanked God for the many blessings He has given us, we would have no time left for anything else. That is how good God is and how much He has blessed us. To say that God is good is a colossal understatement.

I thought about God's goodness and blessings on my life and wondered what would happen if I did this exercise at least once a week. What would happen if I started to name His blessings one by one? Try it. Consider the blessings you have received and start to name them. You will find that something quite interesting happens. Your pace changes. Your perspective starts to switch, and you want less of yourself and more of God. Your attitude also changes. You become a better thanker. When this happens, you grow a little closer to God.

So the next question I pondered was, why aren't we better thankers? This issue goes straight to our nature. We are born selfish, we grow up selfish, and we remain selfish. That is our natural state. We need the supernatural to make us more thankful. The Enemy works to keep us selfish. He tries to keep us focused on ourselves so that we can't see the goodness of God. He is sneaky about this and will resort to low blows whenever he feels the urge. Another of his tricks is to keep us so busy that we can't recognize God's blessings and brush right over them when they come.

The Enemy will also keep us so preoccupied with our own lives that we are not aware when others are struggling. That scenario usually goes like this. A friend tells me he is feeling under the weather and has this and that wrong with him. My response is immediately self-driven, and so I say, "Yeah, well I've got this and that wrong with me, which is worse than what you're going through, so suck it up. I have more problems than you. I win." How silly is that? I know that is not how everyone behaves, but I think it is the natural way to respond. The supernatural way is to listen with empathy and to pray for the friend, to rejoice with those who rejoice and to feel sad with those who feel sad. That is the supernatural way, the Jesus way. We must be a part of the other person's solution rather than ignoring how he feels because we think we feel worse. We must be wise to the tricks of the Enemy. He is good at his job. However, Jesus is better at His.

How do we recognize these tricks and avoid falling prey to them?

The answer as always is the Word of God. He gives us the answer to every problem ever encountered by man. He gives us all the teachings we need for life. People have often told me, "I try to read the Bible, but I just don't understand it. What is stopping me from understanding God's Word?" I have wondered the same thing. There may be an easy answer. God wants all of me, so if I am involved in some kind of sin that I won't give up because it is too much fun, then I am not likely to understand His Word, at least not the deeper meanings.

Another problem is ignoring the Holy Spirit. Perhaps you feel drawn to read God's Word or feel led to talk to someone about something spiritual, but you say, "I will do that later on today when I am settled at home and in my comfies." You pray to be closer to God, but your actions may not line up with your prayers. As in any relationship, the more you ignore and distance yourself from someone, the further that person will drift away from you, straining your ties.

Doubting God's Word will also hinder understanding, playing into the Enemy's hands. You may read a passage and think, *I wish that could be true for my life.* That is what doubt says, and that is what the Enemy wants you to think. Every time you doubt God's Word, that is a point for the Enemy. When you believe God's Word by faith, you crush the Enemy under your feet. The more you do this, the more you grow in faith. You must make the Bible a part of your lifestyle and say, "No matter what, God's Word is true for me. God's Word is real for me. God's Word is power for me. God's Word is living and active for me, and it is sharper than any double- edged sword. God's Word is the bomb." With God's Word you can blow up the Enemy's plan.

So how do you position yourself to understand God's Word? You must live the way God's Word says you should. You must ask God to show you any sin in your life and then turn away from it. Then you will grow in the grace and the knowledge of your Lord and Savior Jesus Christ to whom be glory both now and forevermore. You have an advantage over everyone who lived before the time of Jesus. When Jesus left, He gave us His Spirit so that we may discern how to live as He wants us to live. This Spirit will lead you into all truth. When you read God's Word, you can be assured that truth will be revealed and that the truth will be for you.

My prayer is that you will grasp this idea and read your Bible in the power of the Holy Spirit. Then you will see truth and light. You will recognize every trick of the Enemy before you get wrapped up in one of his cons. You will say, "Ah, I see what you are doing. That is not going to work on me, not this time. This time I know that what God has said in His Word is for me, and I can crush you under my feet. You are no match for my Savior King. Jesus is His name. Yeah, that's right. You know Him, and you shudder in fear at His name. I am His, and He is mine. Thank God Almighty."

Press on...

The Big Question: What Is God's Will for My Life?

After more than a quarter of a decade of seeking God, I have finally figured out what His will is for my life. I used to think God's will for me was tied to what I do for a living. I have recently concluded that God's will starts not with what I do but with who I am. I have prayed for many years for God to reveal His will for me (to tell me what to do), and all the while the answer was right in front of me. God's will for me is not found in the big events of my life. In fact, the way I live my everyday life determines my response to these events. In His Word, God spells out His will, His commands, and His promises for me.

I discover God's will for me in our continual conversation through His Word. His will is not an event or a career. These may make up the good works that God has prepared in advance for me, but they are not the be-all-and-end-all of His will. What if God's will for me right now is to offer Him myself every day, to maintain a great attitude regardless of my circumstances, and to take advantage of every opportunity that presents itself? What if being in His presence day by day, hour by hour, moment by moment, is His will for me? What if I stopped looking to the big picture to discern whether I am in God's will and started looking to the little pictures? What if God's will was a collage of little pictures rather than the big picture? What would life look like then? How would I approach a life that was strictly about the little pictures? The irony is that the big picture is simply a sum total of the little pictures. Since that is the case, I need to stop waiting for the big picture and start living in the mundane. I must start seeing God there. How can I live out God's will in that scenario?

I found the answer in the Bible, which says, "Rejoice always, pray continually, give thanks in all circumstances, for this is God's will for you in Christ Jesus" (1 Thessalonians 5:16–17 NIV).

That's God's will for me. As I reflected on this passage, I was saddened at first because I decided that I would never be in God's will. I am terrible at rejoicing always and praying continually, and I am even worse at giving thanks in all circumstances. I thought, *If that is God's will for me, then I am in trouble.* But I reflected some more and realized that at the end the passage says that is God's will for me "in Christ Jesus." There it is again, the "in Christ Jesus" clause. When I wrote about the mystery of the gospel, the same thing kept coming up. The mystery was Christ in me, the hope of glory. Adding all these thoughts together, I realized that when I fully surrender my life to God, I gain this status of Christ in me. This means I do not have to do everything on my own, because Jesus is living His life through me.

There is no way I can rejoice always, pray continually, or give thanks in all circumstances, but when I reflect on the fact that Christ is alive in me, my whole mood changes and suddenly I see that I can do all things through Christ who strengthens me. As I reflected more on this idea, I became more hopeful. I took this a step further and reflected on what it means to live out of this great hope. I realized that if I am fully surrendered to Christ, He can live through me, so it is no longer I who lives but Christ who lives in me. So I must fully surrender every area of my life—the good, the bad, and the ugly. I must do if I am to have a shot at Christ living His life through me.

I reflected on what it means to be fully surrendered. Here is what I came up with. When Jesus was on this earth, He gave up His life to do nothing but seek God's will and fulfill His desires. That is why Jesus often went off by Himself. He needed to spend time in total surrender to the Father. He probably needed time away from all the ugliness He saw. Jesus depended on His Father entirely while He walked this earth in human form. Just as Jesus fully surrendered to the Father's will, I must empty myself of self and allow His agenda to permeate my being. I am to do nothing but seek the will of Christ for my life. That is total surrender. Then I can live the life I was created to live. If this total surrender is to be mine, I must be completely dependent on Jesus to live His life through me. When I take this approach, my thinking tends to be much clearer. I understand God's Word much more, and I go where I know God is leading me.

Jesus came to breathe his Spirit in us, to make us find our highest happiness in living entirely for God, just as He did. This is what it means to walk as Jesus walked. We are commanded to do this. That requires absolute surrender to the will of the Father. That is the starting point. We must understand that Jesus did nothing apart from His Father's will.

The need for total surrender is a make-or-break point. I can respond to this truth in two ways. I can say, "I don't get this whole business of Christ living in me. Does that mean He is causing me to walk where I walk? Don't I still lead the way? I am human, and I still control my body. This stuff is too hard to understand, so I will go about my life leading the way, surrendering to God's will only when it is beneficial to me. Besides, I am not really in love with God. I am in love with the stuff He does for me and gives me." That is one approach.

There is another. I can lay my whole life in front of God and say, "Search me, God. Help me to know what is offensive to You. Help me to do better. I give myself to You in total surrender.

Continue to teach me what it means to walk as You walked. Continue to teach me what it means for You to live inside of me. Continue to show me Your truth. Continue to use me in this world as You want to use me. Continue to help me to work out this mystery, this hope of glory, which is Christ in me. Thank You that You have chosen to live Your life through me. I am open to whatever, whenever, and wherever. Thank You that I can rejoice always, pray continually, and even give thanks in all circumstances because it is no longer I who lives but You, Jesus, who lives in me.

I will press on till Christ is fully realized in me.

DEEP SPIRITUAL THOUGHT #637

The Real Call of the Wild

Here are questions that have been on my mind for quite some time now: who's will am I really in, and what is the call of God? These are tough questions because if I am being completely honest with myself and with God, I sometimes tend to seek God's blessings and all the good things He has for me and my family, but I live according to my own will and my own desires. I like the word *paradox*. I think it is a neat word to say. I also like the word *juxtaposition*., But enough about the words I like. A paradox is something that seems absurd but could be true.

It certainly seems absurd that I could seek God's blessings but live in my own will. However, at times that is a sad reality.

This is a paradox. I long to live a great Christian life, seeking nothing but the heart of God, but then I catch myself having all kinds of selfish desires and temporal wants. This is a scandalous paradox. I also catch myself trying to fit my Christian walk into my life. Shouldn't my Christian walk be my life?

Then I think, *I must try harder.* I quickly see the error in this method. I realize I won't succeed in my Christian walk simply by trying harder to use the gifts that God has given me for His work. My skills and talents won't suffice. I must rely on what God has put in me. He created me in His image and placed His nature in me when I accepted Him. Trying harder with my gifts is futile. I will fail every time. I must discover who I am as a result of what God has placed in me and learn how His nature is to be lived out through me.

That starts with recognizing the real call of the wild.

Some people say they have the call of the wild, meaning they believe nature is in them and they are happiest when they are in the wilderness or in the jungle. They say this is a part of their nature, something that calls them from within. Another such call is the call of the sea. I grew up in Newfoundland, and I have heard it said that Skipper Jarge has the call of the ocean in him. The sea and the salt air seem to be in his bones, a part of who he is, a part of his nature. He has to be out in a boat, fishing. Usually guys like this make their living from the ocean. They can predict the waters. They seem to have a sixth sense about them. They can navigate through rough spots, because they feel the ocean is a part of them. It is in their nature. I can feel a juxtaposition coming on.

This is like the call of God. To hear the call of God, I must have His nature in me. When the fisherman hears the call of the sea, he responds. When I hear the call of God, I also need to respond. Herein lies the problem. If I am caught in the aforementioned paradox, then I am not likely to hear the call. What is the solution?

I believe it is twofold.

I must first be open to the call of God, even if it doesn't sound appealing. At first glance it seems like God's call to Jesus was a disaster. He called His Son to leave the throne room. When I am comfortable on my couch, I sometimes find it hard to get up. I cannot even imagine having to leave a throne room in heaven to come down to earth to be ridiculed, persecuted, beaten, and killed, and all the while have to listen to a bunch of whiny disciples who were supposed to take over and build the church. That doesn't seem like much of a call. Walking toward the cross doesn't sound too appealing, so I become fearful of God's call, knowing the disappointment and disaster it might bring. And what about the disciples and their call? They too were called to lives of persecution, pain, and suffering, and were eventually killed in horrific ways. Their call was not appealing either. From a human standpoint, it seems that the lives of Jesus and His disciples were failures. However, in God's eyes, their lives were a success. They went exactly as planned and produced priceless results for eternity.

The second part of the solution is understanding that the call of God is not for some specific job; rather it is a call to exercise the nature of God that is in us. Just as fishermen respond to the call of the sea, we must respond to the call of God from within. He calls us to a relationship with Himself that is so intimate that His nature forms our nature and we become synchronized with His will and His desires. This solves the problem of wanting to live the Christian life on our own terms. The more our nature gives way to His nature, the more we become like Him. The more we become like Him, the more we hear His voice and follow His leading in day-to-day activities.

God's call is an invitation to get to know Him more. The more we know Him, the easier it is to recognize what He wants from us. Then we will know how He wants us to use the gifts He has given us. Remember that the call of God can be heard only by those who have His nature. The call is to a relationship so intimate that His nature guides us. We are in His presence for His purpose. He then works out His purpose through us. That is the real call of the wild.

I want more of God's nature in me. I am tired of the "try harder" approach to Christianity. I no longer want what self wants. Jesus, is there anything in me that is not according to Your will and Your call? Show me. Is there something that isn't totally surrendered to You, even something seemingly insignificant?

Show me. Is there anything in my life that isn't from You but is motivated by self? Show me.

I humbly come before You with an empty heart, an open heart, and a willing heart. May You fill my heart with Your nature and Your agenda, and may I come to understand the real call of the wild—because a life totally surrendered to You is wild!

Press on to the wild life.

DEEP SPIRITUAL THOUGHT #664

No Matter What

I want more of God. The pattern seems to be that I get close to Him, feel His presence for a little while, and then wake up the next morning after a great day with God and feel nothing but apathy. Worse yet, I feel as if God has left the building. I studied that pattern and concluded that what I am seeking is more of those feelings—the warm fuzzies or the cold shivers. I thought, *That is the problem. I want more feelings. I want to feel God's presence more. How do I do that?* And then it hit me, that aha moment. I realized what faith was. I concluded that faith was more about knowing God's presence than about feeling God's presence. The feelings just intensify the knowing. The Bible tells me this over and over, but unless I feel God's presence I am not too convinced, so I need reaffirmation through feelings.

There is another problem. As Christians we become absent-minded. We quickly forget God's goodness, the way He has shown up in the past, the miracles we have witnessed. We forget because we always want to feel. We are a feeling people by nature. A lot of people make major decisions based on how they feel or on what kind of mood they are in. I know the feeling. I too fall into the trap of having to be validated based on feelings. The longer I forget, the more I base life on feelings. I tend to treat a lot of relationships according to my feelings. If I am feeling loved, I share love. If I am feeling angry, I may lash out. If I am feeling sad, I become disinterested or distant. If I am feeling happy, perhaps I tell jokes or sing.

I have come to realize through all of this thinking and observing that I need to know God's presence in addition to feeling it. Feelings have a time and a place, but I need to recognize the knowings. The Bible tells me repeatedly about a God who is always with me, a God who will never leave me or forget about me, a God who loves me no matter what. So I have learned that when I don't feel God's presence, I still know God's presence. The same can be said for other relationships. Do you know your wife loves you, or do you constantly need feelings? Once again, feelings play a role, but so does knowing.

I no longer ask, "Why can't I feel God's presence?" I now declare, "God is with me no matter what!" Isn't that incredible? I get to be in relationship with a "no matter what" God. That is mind-blowing. So, as I go to work today, I know that God is walking before me. I know that no matter what happens, I can lean on, look to, and pray to Him. This shift in thinking has been quite a breakthrough. Now when I don't feel His presence, I put faith into action and I know that God is with me no matter what. When I go through sad or happy times, God is with me, no matter how I feel.

Even in my darkest times, God is with me. I recently had an experience that tested my "no matter what" faith. I had blood work done and the doctor thought I had a low-grade lymphoma. So the big *C* was knocking on my door. Where was God now? Turns out He was right there with me every step of the way, giving me a peace that passes all understanding—a peace that I couldn't muster. It came from my "no matter what" God. I was referred to a hematologist to confirm what the issue was. He told me I did not have lymphoma, but I did have early chronic lymphocytic leukemia, which is quite similar. That didn't sound too great either. That is what I thought at first. Then I had a different thought. I could look at this one of two ways. The first was to say, "Well, I guess it's inevitable. I'll just wait until the leukemia is full blown." Doctors do not treat early CLL. Instead they have patients check back six months after diagnosis. They call this the wait-and-watch period. This method could have me living in fear for six months.

However, because I serve a "no matter what" God, I figured I would look at this situation differently. Since my lymphocyte counts weren't quite high enough to call this leukemia, in my mind, I don't have the disease, and I have been given a second chance. Did it occur to me that the end might be near? Absolutely. I wouldn't be human if it didn't. But because I serve a "no matter what" God, I felt His presence throughout this process. I sensed that everything would be okay but that I had work to do. God would do His part, and I would do mine. *Okay,* I thought, *what's my part?*

Since I didn't want to take the fear approach to this ordeal, I thought I would take the faith approach. My part was to do what I could to help my situation and to turn it around in the next several months. I asked the hematologist what he thought, and he suggested alkalizing my body. I wondered if he wanted me to take lots of Alka Seltzer. I didn't know what he meant. I did research and learned that all the foods we eat have a pH level that indicates acidity or alkalinity in our bodies. I discovered that an acidic body is a sick one and that disease apparently cannot live in an alkaline body. I discovered what kinds of food were highest in acidity and was heartbroken when I learned that beef, seafood, soda pop, and coffee were at the top of the list. That was my diet. I learned that a healthy diet is 60 percent alkaline and 40 percent acid. Mine was more like 95 percent acidic. Here I was a seafood-loving, steak-eating, coffee-drinking Newfie who apparently loves all acidic foods.

After the shock wore off and following much prayer, I decided I could accept the path I was on, or I could change my future. Thanks to my awesome wife, who researched meals for the alkaline diet, I finally had something to eat besides vegetables or sprouted bread. I had bio-organic whole-grain spelt fusilli with broccoli and sunflower seeds and a side salad of kale and sprouts. Yes, I said it. Now here is the real kicker and a confession. I kinda liked it. I thought, *Wow! There is life after steak and seafood and breads and burgers and fries. There is spelt and quinoa and sea vegetables and lots of other neat alkalizing foods.* I have my role. I work hard at alkalizing my body, and the "no matter what" God plays His role and prevents this disease from becoming full-blown. You can believe that?

So the next time I start feeling apathetic toward my faith, my health, or anything else, I need to remind myself of three words: no matter what. Faith is above feeling. It is knowing, no matter what.

"The Lord is my shepherd; I have all that I need … He renews my strength … Even though I walk through the darkest valley, I will not be afraid, for you are close beside me [no matter what] … My cup overflows with blessings … Surely your goodness and unfailing love will pursue me [even chase me down] all the days of my life, and I will live in the house of the Lord forever. So be it! (Excerpted from Psalm 23 NLT, brackets mine).

Press on...

DEEP SPIRITUAL THOUGHT #806

Getting to Know You

I was recently reading an article and was reminded of the theological term *prevenient grace*. Simply stated, this means before we can seek God, He must have first sought us. God does a work of enlightenment in us before we start thinking right thoughts about Him. This work is a drawing of the Holy Spirit. It is a sense that we need something more in our lives. It is a realization that there is a void in our hearts and our souls that can be filled only with God. That is prevenient grace. Once God reveals Himself to us, our job is to pursue Him with all we have. I love the psalmist's description of seeking God.

"As the deer longs for water, so I long for you, O God" (Psalm 42:1 NLT). This gives the idea of my whole being craving God just as a deer craves water. The only thing that will satisfy my craving for more of God is more of God. Prevenient grace says God does the drawing first, and then I must act on that. I long to be filled with a longing for more of God.

Something weird has taken place in North American Christianity, a paradox if you will. We have become a little lukewarm when it comes to seeking after the heart of God. What the world needs now is love, sweet love displayed through the person who is desperately seeking after the heart of God just as the deer craves water.

There are levels of seeking. When the term *seeker sensitive* was used to describe a church style, it applied to a church that was designed to help people who were searching for God to find Him. Shouldn't that be all churches? When people were converted or "saved," apparently they had graduated from seeker status. I think the term *seeker* should be synonymous with the term *Christian*. I am a seeker. I seek more of God. I will always be a seeker.

I see this pattern of seekers after the heart of God throughout the Bible. Moses was a God seeker. He wanted to know God better, so he prayed that he would find grace in God's sight and that he might know God. Then Moses made a daring request. He said, "God, I implore you, show me your glory." Now that is bold. How would God respond to such a request? He must have been pleased, because the next day on the mount, His glory passed before Moses. The prophet's prayer to know God more was heard and answered. God wants us to pursue Him and want to know Him more. Moses already knew God, but he was a seeker and wanted to know more of God, so he kept seeking.

Can we ever know too much of God? Can we seek too much?

David was in love with God, and seeking more of the Lord is a theme throughout the book of Psalms. The Psalms ring with the cry of the seeker and the glad shout of the finder. Throughout the Bible we see examples of people who knew God but wanted to know Him more. Those we call the seekers. I seek to be a greater seeker yet.

Just as Moses knew God when he said he wanted to see God's glory, Paul already knew Christ when he said he wanted to know Him. Paul meant that he wanted to know all of Christ, including the power of His resurrection, and to participate in His sufferings. When we are willing to participate in someone's suffering, we have a strong desire to know that person more.

Paul had a burning desire to know Christ. That's how it is when we love someone. We want to know more and more about that person and are willing to share in the suffering as well as the glory. Many Christians would say, "I want to know Christ more and learn about the power of his resurrection. That would be really cool." However, they forget about the suffering part.

It is something to be fully surrendered to Jesus Christ and to know Him intimately to the point of sharing in His sufferings. That is part of what it means to be in God's presence. It is not all rainbows and sunshine. Think about all the Christians around the world even now who are being persecuted and even killed for their faith. They want to know Christ more and are willing to share in His sufferings so they can one day know the power of His resurrection.

In North America we have different issues, and our suffering will not look the same, but the question remains: am I willing to share in Christ's suffering, whatever that may look like for me?

Everything comes down to being in God's presence. By His grace, He gives us the strength to endure suffering. When you have been in God's presence, you are satisfied but left longing for more. You thirst to be made thirsty. Everything else pales in comparison. Oh, to know You more, Jesus. That is my prayer.

> Yes, everything else is worthless when compared with the infinite value of knowing Christ Jesus my Lord. For his sake I have discarded everything else, counting it all as garbage, so that I could gain Christ and become one with him. I no longer count on my own righteousness through obeying the law; rather, I become righteous through faith in Christ. For God's way of making us right with himself depends on faith. I want to know Christ and experience the mighty power that raised him from the dead. I want to suffer

with him, sharing in his death, so that one way or another I will experience the resurrection from the dead! (Philippians 3:8–11 NLT)

So be it.
Press on...

DEEP SPIRITUAL THOUGHT #162

The Ultimate Irony

I have been asking myself a serious question that has major ramifications depending on how I answer it: what is my biggest hindrance to having more of God? After all, I must draw close to God if I want Him to reciprocate. My main struggle is the same one most Christians have today. God originally had first place in our hearts, but sin entered the picture and the things that He created for our pleasure started to become our gods. This is a tale of great irony wrapped up in a perplexing paradox. Could this be true? Are we so stupid that we could let the things God created for our pleasure become our gods?

The answer is no, we are not that stupid, but sin is sneaky. Our shift in allegiances doesn't happen overnight. It is a slow and subtle process. We don't give God first place in our lives and then wake up one morning and say, "I love money and I want more and more of it. In fact, money has become my replacement god" or "I crave power and I want more and more of it. I have decided to worship this new god." The gods we adopt over time could include food, sex, the Internet, hobbies, sports, TV, working out, dancing, drinking, cars, movies, or even working. These are good on their own and in moderation, but whatever is taking the rightful place of God in our hearts can easily become our god. We serve a jealous God, and His first commandment is, "You shall have no other gods before me" (See Exodus 20:3.)

With the fall, we removed God from the center of our hearts and replaced Him with the things He created for us to enjoy, and that is the ultimate in irony. We need to be aware of just how subtle and sneaky this process is. We can recognize our guilt through self-reflection and by asking God to search our hearts. Then we must turn again to Jesus and allow Him first place in our hearts, accepting all the good gifts that He gives us simply as "stuff" and nothing more.

My checkup prayer is always for God to search me and to show me what I value most in my heart. Once stuff is exposed, as it usually is, I ask God to help me do better and to fill those spaces with His presence. I want Him to shine His light in my heart so I in turn can become the light to the world that I was meant to be. Then I can shed light on this issue to others. I don't think I am alone in these struggles. I think we fail to see that things have taken over where God was designed to dwell. Our hearts were meant for God and not for the stuff He created.

The spiritual trouble of the day is rooted in this issue. Material things have become necessities to us, something God never intended. God's gift is now taking the place of God Himself, the ultimate in irony. The course of nature is upset by this sinful substitution. Cell phones are an obvious example. They were meant to aid us but have gone on to become one of our gods. One study finds that people check their smartphones an average of 150 times a day. That number seems excessive to me, but whatever the correct figure, it is for sure a lot. You might want to see for yourself. How many times do you check your smartphone in a day? I know I look at mine more often than needed. So am I saying smartphones are evil? Absolutely not. I love mine, and I use it for many things. I am saying that we should be careful not to move God aside to make room for our creature comforts.

Once we have filled our hearts with all of our stuff, we leave little room for God.

During this conversation with myself, I was reminded of the harsh words of Jesus.

"Then Jesus said to his disciples, Whoever wants to be my disciple must deny themselves and take up their cross and follow me. For whoever wants to save their life will lose it, but whoever loses their life for me will find it. What good will it be for someone to gain the whole world, yet forfeit their soul? Or what can anyone give in exchange for their soul?'" (Matthew 16:24–26 NIV).

The self life leads to the loss of life. We need to turn our backs on the self life and replace it with the God life. In this passage, Jesus calls the cross the only effective way to deal with the self life, the habit of placing stuff above God. That's because the cross denotes death. Jesus says that to follow Him we must deny ourselves and take up our cross—dying to our selfish nature.

We must be willing to give up the things that we think are important to our happiness and put them in their rightful place, at the foot of the cross. This doesn't mean we must get rid of all the toys we own. Rather, we must put them under God's rule for His use. We need to remember that God gives us all these gifts to help us, and we must be thankful. These things are meant as tools and should be secondary in our lives. We need to place God at the center of our hearts for our benefit and for His glory. That is His home.

"You, God, are my God, earnestly I seek you; I thirst for you, my whole being longs for you, in a dry and parched land where there is no water. I have seen you in the sanctuary and beheld your power and your glory. Because your love is better than life, my lips will glorify you. I will praise you as long as I live, and in your name I will lift up my hands. I will be fully satisfied as with the richest of foods; with singing lips my mouth will praise you" (Psalm 63:1–5 NIV). So be it!

Press on...

DEEP SPIRITUAL THOUGHT #774

What Time Is It?

I have been thinking a lot about time and more specifically about what I do with mine. That's easy. I get up, go to work, hit the gym, eat (quinoa and spelt), and engage in other routine activities. But what do I do with my time during periods when I am relentlessly pursuing God and waiting? And how am I waiting? How do I pursue God during those times?

I get bored easily and try to make things happen in the waiting. That is my natural response during periods of waiting. I try to force into being things that aren't there or aren't intended by God. Perhaps these things will come into being a little later and on God's time, but it isn't the right time now. So I wait. I am learning now how to effectively pursue God and to wait on Him at the same time. That may seem like a contradiction, but there is much truth in that statement. The problem is that I am not a good waiter. I need more of the fruit of the Spirit known as patience.

What am I to be doing in the periods of waiting? I believe waiting is part of the journey and could also be called "living life now." Some also refer to these times when nothing seems to be happening as dry periods. These could be times for actively waiting on God. These dry periods are important because they make the close encounters with God stand out all the more. But what do I do in these times?

One approach to take when there is nothing happening, or when you believe God is taking a break or isn't at work in your life, is to take the bull by the horns, kick down some doors, and make something happen. *Don't wait your life away,* you might tell yourself. *Act now. Do something, anything—now! Time is moving on with or without you. Get moving and shaking, you mover and shaker.* That certainly describes my natural approach to life, but in practicing God's presence I have learned that there is a better way.

The first observation I have made is that I am supposed to wait with hope. God can do anything, anytime, any place. Do I have a sustained hope in my waiting or in my everyday living? My hope is that God is leading me into a future that He has planned for me, one much better than I could ever have imagined. Then I observed that I am supposed to wait or to live my everyday life with faith that God will bring me spiritual growth and guide my every step. My next observation is that I must wait with contentment, because godliness with contentment is great gain, according to what God tells me in His Word.

When I don't heed my own observations and God's Word, and I take matters into my own hands, I usually self-destruct. This passage got me thinking about the world's mentality.

"But mark this: There will be terrible times in the last days. People will be lovers of themselves, lovers of money, boastful, proud, abusive, disobedient to their parents, ungrateful, unholy, without love, unforgiving, slanderous, without self-control, brutal, not lovers of the good, treacherous, rash, conceited, lovers of pleasure rather than lovers of God— having a form of godliness but denying its power. Have nothing to do with such people" (2 Timothy 3:1–5 NIV).

That is quite a description of what will happen in the last days, the time between Christ's resurrection and his return in glory. This list describes the people of the world today. It also describes what tends to happen when I take matters into my own hands or let self rule. At least that is the danger.

There is a better way to live. I read further in Timothy and saw the way I am supposed to behave, and that is to "flee the evil desires of youth and pursue righteousness, faith, love and peace, along with those who call on the Lord out of a pure heart" (2 Timothy 2:22 NIV).

When Paul writes about pursuing these things, he is talking about the characteristics of God. So when we pursue God we are pursuing righteousness, faith, love, and peace. We see Paul say something similar in 1 Timothy:

"But you, man of God, flee from all this, and pursue righteousness, godliness, faith, love, endurance and gentleness. Fight the good fight of the faith. Take hold of the eternal life to which you were called when you made your good confession in the presence of many witnesses" (1 Timothy 6:11–12 NIV).

When Paul says "flee from all this," he is referring to the temptations that come from pursuing money. The list of what to pursue as we are waiting or living out our everyday lives includes righteousness, godliness (characteristics like those mentioned here), faith, love, endurance, and gentleness. We take hold of the eternal life to which we were called when we start living out these godlike qualities.

When I say I am pursuing God relentlessly, it means that I am pursuing righteousness. I am also pursuing faith, love, peace, godliness, endurance and gentleness.

This sounds a lot like the fruits of the Spirit, which are love, joy, peace, patience, kindness, goodness, gentleness, faithfulness, and self-control.

When we pursue these, we are pursuing God relentlessly. When we pursue these, we leave little time to be brought down by negativity or by the Enemy, because our minds are fixed on God and godlike qualities. If we can remember this in our times of boredom or of waiting or when nothing seems to be happening, we gain the victory. To check ourselves in these times, we can ask some simple questions. Am I showing love today? What about joy? Am I peaceful or do I need to spend time in prayer? How am I doing in these areas? The more aware we become, the more light we receive. The more light we receive, the more peace we receive. The more we pursue God and the things in His Word, the more we become like Him. And that is the ultimate goal, to become more and more like Jesus.

The great news is that God does all the work. We can't grow in godliness on our own strength, so thank God that He does the work for us. "For God is working in you, giving you the desire and the power to do what pleases Him" (Philippians 2:13 NLT).

Press on...

DEEP SPIRITUAL THOUGHT #864

Sin

Today's thoughts are not for the faint of heart. Read at your own risk!

I was driving down the road the other day and observed something quite interesting. Lately I have been reflecting on many things. It seems when you have a health scare and aren't sure what the outcome will be, you think a little differently. At least that has been my experience since I was told about my early chronic lymphocytic leukemia. On the roadside I saw a person who had let himself go. He was extremely overweight to the point of having a difficult time walking. I thought, *How do we let ourselves get there?* Then I turned the question inward and thought about how I allow myself to get out of shape and overweight. I use all the excuses in the book. I am busy, have kids, there's no time to cook, the job is stressful, and my all-time favorite: I don't have any other vices, so I can eat junk food. At least I am not using comparisons as I once did to make myself feel better about my poor choices.

I have been asking God to show me things in my life that are not pleasing to Him. This means sin. He has showed me my eating habits, my attitude, and other areas that I need to work on. That got me thinking about sin. This subject isn't discussed much these days, but we must avoid sin if we want to get closer to God or practice His presence. I started praying, "God, show me my sin. Search me and know me. Point out where I am falling short. Give it to me." God does show me my sin when I ask. I used to pretend I didn't have sin. I wasn't making light of it, but I was unaware and ignorant.

The person I observed walking down the road opened my eyes to the fact that I was made in God's image and forced me to ask why I allowed myself to eat the way I did, knowing that my body is a temple of the Holy Spirit. Again, I justified my actions. I used every excuse in the book and added more. I became an expert at justifying my sin rather than being honest with myself. It is scary how good I became at this. When I started practicing His presence, I prayed to God to show me a better way, and He has been showing me where I've gone wrong. He has been shining light on areas of my life that He isn't pleased with. Now that I have received light, I have become responsible for doing something about the problem. God made a few additional points to me when I became open to Him and to His leading.

The first thing He made clear was that sin, even seemingly little stuff like lying, puts a wrench in our relationship. Eating whatever I want whenever I want is also sin. I learned that I was to use food as fuel and that fast food was "not fit," as we would say in Newfoundland. God showed me that sin draws me away from His presence. My goal was to be closer to Him. He also showed me that sin hurts Him. I thought, *That's deep. My sin hurts God. Wow! We really do serve a relational God.* He said our relationship was like a husband-and-wife partnership. The two are deeply in love, but ugly sin enters the picture and one partner sins against the other. This draws them apart and damages the relationship. Depending on the extent of the sin, the damage may be beyond repair. The person doing the sinning usually ends up embarrassed and feeling unworthy of love, so he or she pulls away, leaving a huge mess to clean up. God showed me that this is what happens when I sin against Him. I get embarrassed, feel like I don't deserve His love or grace, and I pull away. Sin is like that. It divides; it tears apart; it is ugly; it is the opposite of love. It is above all selfish. In that moment of sin, self takes over (because we allow it to), and that is what drives us away from God.

The great news is that there is a remedy for this ugly sin, however bad or however secret it may be. The remedy is God's love and grace. They are much greater than all my sin. When God reveals my sin to me, I ask forgiveness and seek His help to do better, and He forgives me and forgets about my sin. What an amazing God of grace and mercy! When He forgives me, His love flows again, and I get back on track. The neat thing is that no matter how much I screw up, God is there to restore me, to love me, and to put me back on the right path.

The second thing that God showed me in all of this searching was that I don't want to sin anymore. I am finally at a place in my walk where I don't even like the look of sin. Sin is no longer attractive. The appeal is gone. The closer I get to God, the more I am repulsed by it.

In Romans 7:14–25, Paul discusses the way sin works and how we struggle with it. He talks about wanting to do what is right but failing because of sin living in Him. He does wrong against his will. He wants to do what is good but falls short, again because of sin living in him. He sums up by saying, "Oh what a miserable person I am! Who will free me from this life that is dominated by sin and death? Thank God the answer is in Jesus Christ our Lord" (Romans 7:24–25 NIV).

This passage is about our struggle with sin before finding Christ, but the struggle doesn't stop when we accept Him. We have not arrived. We will arrive only when Christ returns and takes us to be with Him. In the meantime, we have work to do.

We have to stop sinning. That is our job. That seems basic, because it is. When we turn our heads even slightly toward God,

He is there to extend grace. If you are struggling with recurring sin, ask God to expose it, and then ask Him for His grace. You cannot prevail by your own power. You need the blood of Jesus and the power of the Holy Spirit, who is at work within you. That is what God has shown me about the sin in my life, and now I no longer want to sin.

I had to ask two questions. First, do I really want to stop sinning, which appears to be fun? Second, do I just seek to stop sinning or have I stopped? John deals with this topic in a black-and-white fashion.

"Everyone who sins is breaking God's law, for all sin is contrary to the law of God. And you know that Jesus came to take away our sins, and there is no sin in him. Anyone who continues to live in him will not sin. But anyone who keeps on sinning does not know him or understand who he is" (1 John 3:4–6 NLT).

That seems pretty simple. As Christ's followers we have the ability to stop sinning, not just the desire, through the power of the Holy Spirit. One last thing about sin: it is sneaky. Just when we think we are immune, it comes at us in a different form. Remember, as Christ's follower we do not have to give in to sin. We can overcome it.

Here is some good advice from the book of James: "So humble yourselves before God. Resist the devil, and he will flee from you. Come close to God, and God will come close to you" (James 4:7–8 NLT).

Thank You, God, that I am more than a conqueror of sin through Christ Jesus, who loves me.

Press on...

DEEP SPIRITUAL THOUGHT #065

A "Successful" Christian Walk

I have been thinking a lot lately about what is required for a successful Christian walk. I have identified a couple of things, but first I want to define the word *successful*. In the Christian context, it means walking as Jesus walked. I have several questions: What moves the heart of God more than anything else? What has the power to change the course of this world? What are the results of a successful Christian walk?

The answer to these questions is not elusive by any means. It is prayer—not just a "Hey, God, what's up?" kind of a prayer, but a fervent, passionate appeal to a holy God who is just and full of mercy and wants desperately to change our world. Such prayer comes as a result of a close Father-child relationship. Jesus modeled this for us while He walked the earth. He always seemed to be going off on His own to reconnect with the Father in preparation for what would come next. At the beginning of His ministry, He spent forty days in the desert preparing through prayer.

There are no shortcuts when it comes to prayer. Francis Fenelon, a French Roman Catholic archbishop in the seventeenth century, said prayer was the most essential and the most neglected duty of Christians in his day. He said most people thought it was a tiring ceremony and shortened their prayer time as much as possible. He lived from 1651 to 1715, and it seems as if he had a crystal ball. This has been a chronic problem for Christians in all ages. If I am honest with myself, I can see shortcuts I have taken in my prayer life. I also see prayer as a tiring exercise at times. If we look at Jesus, however, we can see that He got His power from prayer. It refreshed and strengthened Him.

I must seek a closer walk with Jesus and much more dependence on the Father through passionate prayer. I have a direct line to God through prayer. I don't have to go through priests or anyone else. The throne room is open for business. I can come boldly to the throne and find grace and mercy. Why don't I take greater advantage of this? I get distracted and I am spiritually lazy to some degree. Those are my issues. God says, "Come in. I will always listen and answer." This direct line to God through prayer turns our impoverishment into wealth. It changes our weaknesses into strengths, our sorrows into joys, our sickness into health. It turns the tables on the state of this world and overturns intended evil. It brings us to the glory of God. What a privilege! Jesus showed us the importance of prayer when He got ticked off at the moneychangers in the temple and knocked over their tables. He said that His Father's house was a house of prayer. Jesus had a direct link to the Father through prayer, and we can have that same access if only we would draw nearer.

What do you think would happen if enough of us started passionately and fervently crying out to God to change our world? If enough of us did that, I dare say we might start a revolution—a prayer revolution that sees us more and more occupied with the things of God and less and less with the things of this world. I have to ask myself whether I want to see that kind of a revolution. Do I want to spend time in the passionate prayer that makes a difference in this world? Are there other Christians who would like to see a revolution that leads to more and more of God and less and less of us? This would mean that God would be dictating how we live, and we would have to loosen our tight control. That would mean a change in how we spend our time each day and a change in our mind-set. We would have to believe that God was our all in all. If enough Christians started a prayer revolution, asking God to change the world, heaven would listen, and we would start to see things happen. The world would probably look like nothing we could imagine, because God would probably do immeasurably more than what we could ask or envision. What if God did not withhold one good thing from us? How would that look? How would the world be changed? What if we gave our souls to God in prayer? What if we trusted Him with everything? What if?

Prayer is also a great way to practice God's presence and to draw near to Him. The closer I get to God through prayer, the more I seem to know His will and how to live my everyday life. The closer I get to God through prayer, the less I want to act out things of the flesh. I still find myself slipping up in fleshly areas, such as having a bad attitude or complaining about things I have no right to complain about, but I am instantly aware when I am closely connected through prayer.

One of the main things to remember about prayer is that we must have patience. Sometimes we see prayer as an instant solution and want to see results as soon as we say amen. This is like a recipe that says, "Just add water," implying you will get immediate results. Prayer is often best measured by looking back in time. My experiment of practicing God's presence was a year in duration. I was going to seek God more intensely than I ever had before, and looking back since that year has elapsed, I can see many incredible answers to prayer. I know that it would have been impossible for me to achieve these results on my own. Every facet of my life has improved as a result. God seemed to be saying, "Thanks for finally submitting in every area. Now step aside and watch what I can do." I wonder what He could do with a group of people who passionately cry out to Him in prayer. I bet it would be immeasurably more than a revolution. That is how God is.

He is an "immeasurably more" God, and He wants to find such a group of people.

God's Word has come alive throughout this past year, and I have claimed many promises in that time. The following two verses were ones I kept returning to over and over again. They have become my life prayer in a way. I pray this prayer for myself, my family, and for all of you.

"May you experience the love of Christ, though it is too great to understand fully. Then you will be made complete with all the fullness of life and power that comes from God. Now all glory to God, who is able, through his mighty power at work within us, to accomplish infinitely more than we might ask or think. Glory to him in the church and in Christ Jesus through all generations forever and ever! Amen" (Ephesians 3:19–21 NLT).

Press on...

Looking Back, Looking Forward, and Looking Up

I must get better at looking back, looking forward, and looking up. I need first to look back at what God has done, at His faithfulness, at His greatness, at His love, mercy, and forgiveness. That is what I learned on day 317 of my 365-day journey of practicing God's presence (which is continuing past 365 days to infinity). Looking back, I can see how God has been present in each stage of my life and how He has rescued me over and over again. How He prevented me from getting involved in things I should not have been involved in. How He inspired me to take a deep long look at myself and where I was spiritually several years ago.

I also see how He instigated situations in my life where I had no choice but to do one thing. He brought me to the point where there were no decisions left to make. The only option was the one God had chosen. I can see that now. God has proven His goodness over and over, and the neat thing is I have all the examples written down. When I started this experiment of practicing God's presence, I began keeping a journal of what God was teaching me and of how He brought me through many difficult situations. I can look back a year later and read about God's goodness. He has shown me that He is indeed a great God who hears our prayers and responds to them. It is good to reflect on what God has done. However, we must not stay in the past. We look forward, and because of the past, I am extremely excited about the future.

Looking forward is a healthy spiritual exercise as long as we do not get so wrapped up in the future that we can't enjoy the present. God willing, it will be a great and glorious future. Looking forward, I pray about God's will for me and my family. How will the gifts and the graces God has given me relate to the future? I know that God wants me to love Him with all my heart, soul, strength, and mind. I am also to love my neighbor as myself. God's Word is clear about this. When I love like this, a whole bunch of benefits follow. With great love come joy, peace, patience, kindness, goodness, gentleness, faithfulness, and self-control. That is God's will for me now and in the future, and it is incredible. What more could I ask for than a life of love, peace, and joy?

Reading Peter this morning in God's Word was the catalyst for these thoughts. He wrote, "God has given each of you a gift from his great variety of spiritual gifts. Use them well to serve one another. Do you have the gift of speaking? Then speak as though God himself were speaking through you. Do you have the gift of helping others? Do it with all the strength and energy that God supplies. Then everything you do will bring glory to God through Jesus Christ. All glory and power to him forever and ever. Amen" (1 Peter 4:10–11 NLT).

So that answers the question about looking forward. I am to use the gifts that God has so graciously given me to serve others. Am I doing that, or am I keeping those gifts to myself? Gifts are given to benefit others. If someone is special to us, we desperately want to find the perfect Christmas gift for that person. We don't buy gifts to benefit ourselves unless we are buying selfishly. If we care about someone, we want the gift to benefit that person. That's exactly how it is with God. He gives us gifts so we can share them with other people, who are also special to Him. He uses us to reach people, and we do this by using our gifts in service to others. We shouldn't use our gifts to make us feel better about ourselves or to feel important. We need a checkup from the neck up if that is the reason we are sharing our gifts. Peter says everything we do will bring glory to God through Jesus Christ if we are using our gifts to benefit others.

Looking up is even more important than looking back and looking forward. Looking up involves several elements. For me, it first means coming boldly to the throne of grace. In Hebrews we read, "So let us come boldly to the throne of our gracious God. There we will receive his mercy, and we will find grace to help us when we need it most" (Hebrews 4:16 NLT).

When I need grace, which seems to be quite often, thank God that He allows me to approach His throne to seek His help. Looking back, I can definitely see the results of approaching God's throne and of seeking His help. Looking forward, I can also say with certainty that wherever He leads me in the future, He will be there to help me each step of the way.

Looking up also means that I need to reflect on heaven more often. The busyness of the world clouds our thoughts and leaves us little time to consider such things. I now realize I have to set aside time for this spiritual exercise. To think that I can come to the throne of our gracious God overwhelms me. When I look up, I have to ask myself, *What do I see? Do I see Isaiah's vision of heaven or John's description of the throne room in Revelation?* I need to get better at looking up so I can see what is described in God's Word. Here is how John describes it.

> After this I looked, and there before me was a door standing open in heaven. And the voice I had first heard speaking to me like a trumpet said, "Come up here, and I will show you what must take place after this." At once I was in the Spirit, and there before

me was a throne in heaven with someone sitting on it. And the one who sat there had the appearance of jasper and ruby. A rainbow that shone like an emerald encircled the throne. Surrounding the throne were twenty-four other thrones, and seated on them were twenty-four elders. They were dressed in white and had crowns of gold on their heads.

From the throne came flashes of lightning, rumblings and peals of thunder. In front of the throne, seven lamps were blazing. These are the seven spirits of God. Also in front of the throne there was what looked like a sea of glass, clear as crystal. In the center, around the throne, were four living creatures, and they were covered with eyes, in front and in back. The first living creature was like a lion, the second was like an ox, the third had a face like a man, the fourth was like a flying eagle. Each of the four living creatures had six wings and was covered with eyes all around, even under its wings. Day and night they never stop saying: "'Holy, holy, holy is the Lord God Almighty,' who was, and is, and is to come."

Whenever the living creatures give glory, honor and thanks to him who sits on the throne and who lives forever and ever, the twenty-four elders fall down before him who sits on the throne and worship him who lives forever and ever. They lay their crowns before the throne and say: "You are worthy, our Lord and God, to receive glory and honor and power, for you created all things, and by your will they were created and have their being." (Revelation 4 NIV)

Reflect on that imagery for a second. Allow your mind to wander. This seems like something out of a science fiction novel, but if you compare this account with Isaiah's, you will see two visions by two people. Isaiah's vision is found in the sixth chapter of the book bearing his name. It is interesting to read that account and then the one in Revelation. Take a look at how these men of God responded to their experiences. Then ask yourself how you would respond if you saw these visions. This is an interesting exercise, and I can relate to Isaiah's reaction: "Woe to me, I cried. I am ruined. For I am a man of unclean lips, and I live among a people of unclean lips, and my eyes have seen the King, the Lord Almighty" (Isaiah 6:5 NIV).

Luckily for us there is grace at the throne, and right away we see this grace in action. As soon as Isaiah says this, an angel flies over to him, holding a live coal that he took with tongs from the altar. He then touches Isaiah's mouth and says, "See, this has touched your lips; your guilt is taken away and your sin atoned for" (Isaiah 6:7 NIV). Grace from the throne room in action. Thank God for His throne and for His grace. Keep looking up!

Press on...

DEEP SPIRITUAL THOUGHT #593

Who Am I?

Have you ever had any of these thoughts? *I am not good enough for … I am not smart enough to … I am not good-looking enough. I do not have enough talent. I can't reach that goal that I desire or do what God wants me to do. I am just not enough.* That seems to be one of the biggest fears that we face today. We think we aren't enough. No matter what confronts us, we don't quite measure up. Worse yet, we aren't as good as so-and-so. We start comparing ourselves to others and that feeds the "not enough" syndrome.

That is apparently the greatest fear in our society, and the second is quite similar: not having enough. No matter how much we have, we are just a little short. If only we could get one more thing and attain the next level. But we always miss it by "that much," as Agent Maxwell Smart used to say. Think about these two statements and see if there is any truth in them. I am not good enough, and I don't have enough. Unfortunately, we usually act in accordance with these fears.

Obviously these are great lies perpetrated by the Enemy, aka Satan. He tries to implant these lies in our minds, hoping we repeat them to ourselves and they get embedded deep enough that they become a part of our belief system. I can imagine Satan and his angels at a board meeting, trying to figure out their next move. Then Mephistopheles says, "Why don't we just keep whispering in their ears things like 'You aren't good enough' whenever we see them trying to accomplish something? If we do that over and over, the idea will take root and cause them much grief." The demons unanimously approve the plan, and this becomes the deadliest arrow in their quiver.

The danger is that you will start to believe that you are not enough or that you do not have enough and will live by these fears. There is a better way: faith.

It is fine and dandy for the devils to have their little plan, because the truth is, if you have accepted Christ and live by His Word, there is now no condemnation. You have been forgiven. You do not need to take your past failures into your future. As Stuart Smalley, a character from *Saturday Night Live,* would say, "I'm good enough, I'm smart enough, and doggone it, people like me." That is exactly right. You are good enough, you are smart enough, and you can do all things through Christ who strengthens you.

The next time Satan comes to you with his nonsense, reminding you of your past and saying you aren't good enough because of this or that, remind him of his future. Also remind him of this verse in Romans: "So now there is no condemnation for those who belong to Christ Jesus" (Romans 8:1 NLT). Tell him, "You can't condemn me. I belong to Jesus, so take that." This is enough to make even the greatest enemy slither away in defeat. The Bible paints the real picture of who we are in Christ. I searched the Word, but I couldn't find any verse telling me I wasn't good enough. In fact, I found the opposite to be true. Here's what I discovered about who I am.

I am a child of God.

I am Christ's friend.

I have been justified.

I am united with the Lord, and His Spirit lives in me.

I have been bought at a price.

I belong to God.

I am a member of Christ's body.

I am a saint.

I have been adopted as God's child.

I have direct access to God through the Holy Spirit.

I have been redeemed and forgiven of all my sins.

I am complete in Christ.

I am free forever from condemnation. There is no more.

I am assured that all things work together for good for those who love God.

I cannot be separated from the love of God.

I have been anointed and sealed by the blood of the Lamb.

My life is hidden with Christ in God.

I am confident that the good work God has begun in me will be completed in Christ Jesus.

I am a citizen of heaven.

I have not been given a spirit of fear but of power, of love, and of a sound mind.

I can find grace and mercy to help in time of need.

I am born of God and am protected from the Enemy.

I am the salt of the earth.

I am the light of the world.

I am a branch of the true vine, and His life flows through me.

My body is God's temple.

I am a minister of reconciliation, telling others who they can be.

I am seated with Christ in the heavenly realm.

I am God's workmanship, made in His image.

I may approach the throne of our gracious God with freedom and confidence.

I can do all things through Christ who strengthens me.

I am more than a conqueror.

I am Christian!

That is who I am. When I am caught in an identity crisis, I need only remember who I am in Christ and my real identity will come to the forefront. So the next time you feel yourself getting caught up in the "not good enough" syndrome, take a minute to read through this short list of who you are in Christ. Reading this list three or four times a day for about a month will change your mind forever. Repetition will embed your true identity in your brain, and when you are in greatest need, you will be able to recall who you are. When the Enemy is whispering that you are not good enough, any amnesia you suffer will be temporary. You will remember who you are and realize there is no condemnation, and you will proceed to tell him all about his future in the abyss.

So remember who you are and …

Press on...

The Secret to Living the Christian Life

The secret to living the Christian life is a paradox because we cannot live the Christian life. Over the years I have asked many people how to live a successful Christian life. More often than not, they have told me to go to church every Sunday, to read the Bible daily, to spend time with God in prayer, to give money to the church and other good causes, or to serve as a volunteer. Do these things, they said, and you will be living a successful Christian life. I started thinking, *That's it? That's the formula for success? I remember the Pharisees, a group of people who lived by a strict set of rules to try to please God and to earn rewards. What happened to those guys? For starters, Jesus called them a brood of vipers.* Then I thought, *All those things, such as praying and reading the Bible, are good on their own, but they do not necessarily help me to live a successful Christian life. In fact, they may even hinder finding success. These elements of the walk must be a byproduct of living the Christian life. I will want to do them because of the overflowing life within me.*

The secret to living a successful Christian life is that you can't. Only when Jesus lives His life through you do you become successful. Jesus must be your example of how to live the Christian life. You can't rely on some TV evangelist, your pastor, or your best friend who seems to have it all together. These people can surely help you in your walk, but your ultimate example must be Jesus. And how did Jesus live the Christian life? First of all, He is the Christian life, but the King of Kings didn't put on airs. Instead He came in humility. He didn't announce to His disciples, "I've got this, guys! Watch this miracle and that one." No. He modeled exactly how to live the successful Christian life. So how did He do that?

Jesus was continually connected with the Father. If Jesus couldn't live a successful Christian life apart from the Father, what makes me think I can? How arrogant could I be? I would be wrong to say, "It's okay, God. I've got this." This attitude is completely contrary to living a successful Christian life. I must heed this verse:

"I have not ever acted, and will not in the future act, on my own. I listen to the directions of the one who sent me and act on these divine instructions. For this reason, my judgment is always fair and never self-serving. I'm committed to pursuing God's agenda and not my own" (John 5:30, The Voice).

That is the kind of Christian I want to be, one so in tune with God's presence that I hear His divine instructions, causing my judgments to be fair and not self-serving. I want to be committed to God's agenda and not my own. All those other things, such as going to church, reading the Bible, and using my gifts and talents, will come about as an overflow of God's presence. That is living the successful Christian life.

I want to be the type of Christian who seeks God's presence, His love, His joy, and His hope and not just His gifts and what He can do for me. I want to connect to God as Jesus did in His life on earth. I want to be in God's presence rather than merely receiving His presents. That is a hard declaration to make because some doubts come with so bold a statement. Do I really seek God's presence rather than His presents? I know that by seeking His presence I will learn how to live like Jesus did. I know that when I am seeking only what I can get out of God and do things on my own strength, I am a colossal failure. Jesus told us that living a life of faith apart from the Father was impossible even for Him. If Jesus couldn't do this in His own strength, why should I even try? I approach some things with ego instead of humility leading the way. That must stop once and for all.

After compiling and sifting through all of these thoughts, I concluded that I need to stop trying to live the Christian life successfully—at least in my own strength. I need to start living the Christian life as it was intended to be lived and as it was modeled for me by Jesus. I need to strive for a more intimate daily practice of checking in with God and waiting on His divine instructions. That is the formula for a successful Christian life. Every good pursuit will flow from the fullness I gain. I will not only want to read the Bible every day, but I will crave it. I will want to be in God's Word, receiving His instructions. I will not want to forsake the assembly as many are in the habit of doing. Rather, I will want to be at church with God's people, and it will hurt when I am away. I will want to do all the other things associated with a successful Christian walk. They will be a natural overflow, because I have learned how to seek God's presence and not just His presents.

Press on to that successful Christian walk.

DEEP SPIRITUAL THOUGHT #821

More than Food?

The question of living out Christianity is still rattling around in this old noggin of mine. I know that I need to stop trying in my own strength if I want to live a successful Christian life. But how is that supposed to happen in my everyday routine? How am I supposed to do this in the world today? I was reminded of the answer while watching a movie last night. The film was about a college freshman who ended up debating his professor about the existence of God. I recalled a verse from one of Peter's letters in which he says we should always be ready with an answer when asked about our faith. Every student in this first-year philosophy class was bullied into denying the existence of God, but one young man would have none of it. He could not deny his faith. He took the following verse to heart:

"But in your hearts revere Christ as Lord. Always be prepared to give an answer to everyone who asks you to give the reason for the hope that you have. But do this with gentleness and respect" (1 Peter 3:15 NIV).

Always be ready with an answer. That tells me I need to dig more into the Word and continue to learn so I will never be stuck without an answer when someone asks me a question about my faith. That's what happened in this movie. People received answers directly from the Word when questions were asked. This theme was repeated throughout the movie with the Christian characters. They had answers to the questions, and they spoke the answers in the form of Scripture. To effectively do this, one must be well versed in the Bible and talk about it often. I wondered, *Do I practice that enough? Do I practice sharing what I have learned from the Word when people ask me questions, or do I keep the answers secular? Do I know enough Scripture to be ready with an answer in every situation?*

Fortunately we have an example of how we should deal with such situations from someone who also lived on this earth. Before Jesus started His ministry, He was led out into the wilderness by the Spirit to pray and to fast. While there He was tempted by Satan, and each time He was tempted, Jesus quoted Scripture as a response. Jesus showed us by example how we are to approach these situations. So not only should we be ready when we are questioned about our faith, but we should also be ready with the Word when our faith is tested. It is in our best interest to know God's Word and to be ready for anything. That is the example Jesus gave us. He not only knew the Scriptures, but He conversed in them.

"Then Jesus was led by the Spirit into the wilderness to be tempted by the devil. After fasting forty days and forty nights, he was hungry. The tempter came to him and said, 'If you are the Son of God, tell these stones to become bread.' Jesus answered, 'It is written: "Man shall not live on bread alone, but on every word that comes from the mouth of God"'" (Matthew 4:1–4 NIV).

We need to be immersed in the Word of God. We need to live on every word that comes from the mouth of God, according to Jesus. No other book ever written has as much significance as the Bible. We are told that the word *Bible* stands for "basic instructions before leaving earth." But the Bible is so much more than basic instructions. It contains all the instructions we could ever need for every area of our lives. It is our complete guidebook while on earth. It is our playbook, our instruction manual, our road map, and sustenance for living.

Imagine a world without Bibles. People in other countries will walk a hundred miles in bare feet to get what we in North America take for granted. They understand that the Word of God is life itself. The next time you walk by a dusty Bible on a shelf, ask yourself, *What is my relationship with God's Word? Am I a skimmer? Am I a "read it when I am in trouble" type of a person? How do I really feel about the Bible?* Journeying through this year, I have come to realize just how important God's Word is in practicing His presence. For Christians, the Bible is food for living a deeper spiritual life.

God's Word gives us strength for living, hope for living, and direction for living. We need bread for physical life, but living the Christian life requires so much more than bread. Jesus said this even after fasting for forty days, and He was certainly quite hungry. Even in this famished state, He said we need God's Word more than we need food, and we all know we need food to survive. We need God's Word to live the life we were meant to live. If we want to connect with God on a deep, intimate level, we need to increase our appetite for His Word. Here is a fun little quiz that offers great insight.

Q: What is the shortest chapter in the Bible?
A: Psalm 117.
Q: What is the longest chapter in the Bible?
A: Psalm 119.
Q: Which chapter is at the center of the Bible?
A: Psalm 118.

There are 594 chapters before Psalm 118. There are 594 chapters after Psalm 118. Add these numbers up and you get 1,188.

Q: What is the center verse in the Bible?

A: Psalm 118:8.

"It is better to take refuge in the Lord than to trust in humans" (Psalm 118:8 NIV).

Right in the center of the Bible, we are told to trust God and His Word rather than to trust people. God will never let us down, and people are ... people.

Does this verse say something significant about God's perfect will for our lives?

When you hear people say they would like to find God's will for their lives and want to be in the center of His will, send them to the center of His Word. His Word is our life.

Press on...

DEEP SPIRITUAL THOUGHT #926

Did Jesus Really Mean It?

What if Jesus meant what He said while on the mount delivering His inaugural address? In Matthew 5–7 we read a great sermon from the greatest teacher ever, but we may suspect that He couldn't possibly have meant some of the things He said. Reading and rereading the Sermon on the Mount, I am convicted almost every time. And how can Jesus tell me not to worry? Who does He think He is talking to? Worry seems to be a full-time occupation in this world today or at least the equivalent of a part-time job. He gives me His instructions in chapter 6, verses 25–34. Jesus sums them up by saying, "So do not worry, saying, what shall we eat? Or what shall we drink? Or what shall we wear? For the pagans run after all these things, and your Heavenly Father knows you need them. But seek first His kingdom and His righteousness, and all these things will be given to you as well. Therefore do not worry about tomorrow, for tomorrow will worry about itself. Each day has enough trouble of its own" (Matthew 6:31–33 NIV).

So why am I convicted about this? I do tend to worry at times about the grocery bill, about clothes, and about bills related to shelter. I worry about these things even though Jesus gave me specific instructions not to fret. I should seek God's kingdom first, and then all these things will be supplied. Looking back, I can see how wonderfully God has provided for me in these areas, so I shouldn't worry about them.

Jesus points to how He takes care of the birds of the air and the flowers and grass of the field and says He cares far more about me. What if Jesus meant what He said?

Jesus also tells me that I should not worry about tomorrow. Doesn't He know that I have that big project due at work tomorrow? Doesn't He know I have that big exam tomorrow? Doesn't He know that I am going to the clinic to get my lab results tomorrow? Doesn't He know that it is my last day of work due to a layoff tomorrow? Doesn't He know about all these things that are supposed to take place tomorrow? Indeed He does. Despite all of His knowledge about tomorrow, He says not to worry, for tomorrow will worry about itself. Each day has enough trouble of its own.

Jesus isn't saying, "Just think positive things, and positive things will come your way" or "Just think about positive things financially, and you will come into wealth." He isn't saying, "Just think healthy thoughts, and there will be no sickness." If these lines are starting to sound like the predominant message from TV evangelists, then I have some disappointing news. That is not the message of Jesus. He says not to worry about tomorrow, because tomorrow will worry about itself. He assures us that each day has enough trouble of its own. Did He really mean that? Are the positive-thinking preachers wrong? What did Jesus really mean?

"But seek first his kingdom and his righteousness, and all these things will be given to you as well. Therefore do not worry about tomorrow, for tomorrow will worry about itself. Each day has enough trouble of its own" (Matthew 6:33–34 NIV).

Jesus is telling us that our minds should be occupied with seeking God's kingdom and His righteousness. We should be seeking to live the way Christ lived. Righteousness comes from a righteous God, and that is to be our top priority. Then all these other things will be added. Yes, tomorrow shouldn't cause concern today because each day has enough problems of its own. Jesus is not saying that if we seek His kingdom we will be free from all the world's problems or that there will be nothing but sunshine, rainbows, lollipops, and an occasional unicorn. He assures us there will be troubles. However, Jesus also assures us that when we go through the troubles of the day He will be walking by our side, step by step. That is His promise to us. What if Jesus meant what He said? Would that change the way we live?

I have been reading lately about St. Francis of Assisi and his approach to Christianity. He had a deep connection with all of nature and an affinity for love and peace. He was one of the first Christian environmentalists. I have been reflecting on his most well-known prayer, which tells us about who he was. St. Francis seemed to live out his prayer. It reads:

> Lord, make me an instrument of thy peace.
> Where there is hatred, let me sow love;
> Where there is injury, pardon;
> Where there is doubt, faith;
> Where there is despair, hope;
> Where there is darkness, light;
> Where there is sadness, joy.
>
> O divine Master, grant that I may not so much seek
> To be consoled as to console,
> To be understood as to understand,
> To be loved as to love.
> For it is in giving that we receive;
> It is in pardoning that we are pardoned;
> It is in dying to self that we are born to eternal life.

This prayer says a lot about who Francis Bernandone was. Many are familiar with his prayer but not so much with what drove and inspired him. He was born in Assisi, Italy, in 1181 or 1182. At the age of twenty-two, after a sudden illness that brought him almost to the point of death, he left his home and his inheritance to follow an instruction that he felt he had received from Christ: Francis, go and rebuild my church.

He went on to start many monasteries and has been admired for almost a thousand years. St. Francis lived his life as if Jesus meant what He said. Lord Chesterton had this to say about the saint: "Francis may have been the last true Christian." The claim is a little dramatic perhaps, but it speaks about how he lived his life. I wonder what they will say about me. What if Jesus meant what He said?

Press on...

DEEP SPIRITUAL THOUGHT #365

What a Difference a Year Can Make

One year! It has now been one year since I made the commitment to set aside time with God to practice His presence and to put the thoughts that I received on paper in the form of a daily journal. Originally I thought, *A year goes pretty fast, so why don't I journal my experiences of finding God?* The year started out quite well as I was receiving lots of insights from God each day. About halfway through I hit a wall, and for the better part of fifty days I felt nothing—no inspiration, no joy, just blasé indifference. I felt no motivation to write, and as I look back on those days I see stuff like blah blah blah written in my journal or nothing at all. This was a wilderness time. I thought I had learned enough at that point, so I started to coast a bit in my faith. I didn't have the same passion for the awareness of Jesus and His daily presence. I wasn't asking myself on a daily basis, *Where is Jesus now? Would He approve of my thoughts and actions?* I was on cruise control, and I needed to kick myself out of it.

When the Holy Spirit revealed to me what was going on, it was as if I had awakened from a bad dream. I was in a rut and the Enemy was digging it, so many arrows were being slung my way. But when I recognized my situation, I grabbed the sword of the Spirit and fought back. I then started receiving more and more insights into who God is and what He does. Looking back over the

238

whole year, I can see clearly what I was doing. I was taking some of Paul's advice when he says: "Therefore, my dear friends, as you have always obeyed—not only in my presence, but much more in my absence—continue to work out your salvation with fear and trembling, for it is God who works in you to will and to act in order to fulfill his good purpose" (Philippians 2:12–13 NIV).

That would be the best way to describe my year. I said I was practicing God's presence, but I was actually working out my salvation with fear and trembling. I was seeking God's presence so He could work in me to will and to act according to His good purpose. My job is to work out my salvation, to work through any sins by the Holy Spirit's leading, and to ask forgiveness. When we do that, God takes over and forgives, restores, and rebuilds us into the people we were created to be. That is His job. If we get out of the way and allow Him to do His work, He gives us the will to cooperate in that work. I know this to be quite true, because I always seem to get in the way. I am really good at it. God shows me continually that His way is much better than mine no matter how much I may fight that. This past year has taught me how God does the work. I have had many high moments but still many struggles with self and with fighting for my way.

I have also had many landmark moments with Jesus. It is still possible today to have these radical times of power. Saul's conversion is a great example of this. Jesus may want to perform miracles through us, but for that to happen we need to be prepared by taking Paul's advice to work out our salvation with fear and trembling. Why fear and trembling? Because when we realize what a powerful God we serve and how big He is, we must show our humility and our awareness of His presence. When we experience a miracle or a powerful time with God, our salvation journey receives enormous encouragement.

We know our salvation will not be made complete until Christ returns, but until that time we need to be aware of His presence and of the ride we are on. Until Christ's return, we remain in a growth pattern. Our growth tends to be gradual so that we can draw closer to God each day and look back and see that growth. This works the same way for any intimate relationship in which we are involved. With my personality, I would prefer to be zapped by Jesus and be as mature as I should be all at once, but that isn't the design. There would be no working out of my salvation with fear and trembling. Looking back, I am grateful that the process is a slow and gradual one, because that is how we grow. We don't come out of the womb one day and wake up fully grown the next. Growth is a slow process that takes time. Our bodies need to work out their growth with nutrients, vitamins, minerals, and proteins. We start with milk and then move gradually to solid food. In the same way, our spiritual growth requires certain things at certain times. Thank God for the way He has worked it all out. We just need to do our part and growth happens.

As I come to the end of this year, I think, *Okay, God, my year of practicing Your presence is over, so what is next?* The obvious answer is that I must continue to work out my salvation with fear and trembling until Jesus returns, perfecting it. Until that happens I will continue to practice His presence. My advice to you is the same advice that I took from Paul one year ago.

"Therefore, my dear friends, as you have always obeyed—not only in my presence, but much more in my absence—continue to work out your salvation with fear and trembling, for it is God who works in you to will and to act in order to fulfill his good purpose" (Philippians 2:12–13 NIV).

And one more piece of advice:

Press on...

The Last Word

Thank you for taking the time to read the thoughts of a fellow pilgrim on a faith journey. I have learned many things about who God is and how He interacts with and responds to me. I hope you have drawn a little closer to Him as a result of your reading. Perhaps you are inspired to take a similar journey, and if that is so, I would love to read about it someday. In case you have been trying to figure out the significance of my numbering system, there is no significance. The thought doesn't necessarily line up with the day. There were many days when I didn't get any inspiring thoughts, so the numbering system is purely random.

I would like to leave you with a little prayer from the apostle Paul. He prayed it to the believers in Ephesus, and I echo his sentiments to all who read this book. May God richly and deeply bless you as you follow Him and practice being in His presence.

> For this reason I kneel before the Father, from whom every family in heaven and on earth derives its name. I pray that out of his glorious riches he may strengthen you with power through his Spirit in your inner being, so that Christ may dwell in your hearts through faith. And I pray that you, being rooted and established in love, may have power, together with all the Lord's holy people, to grasp how wide and long and high and deep is the love of Christ, and to know this love that surpasses knowledge—that you may be

filled to the measure of all the fullness of God. Now to him who is able to do immeasurably more than all we ask or imagine, according to his power that is at work within us, to him be glory in the church and in Christ Jesus throughout all generations, forever and ever! Amen. (Ephesians 3:14–21 NIV)

Press on...

CPSIA information can be obtained at www.ICGtesting.com
Printed in the USA
LVOW07s0821310115

425076LV00001B/24/P